CW00429376

Grundkurs
What is Architecture About?
Pier Paolo Tamburelli

MACK

Devil's Tower Becomes Architecture Because it is Precisely Chosen by the Aliens: An Introduction to the *Grundkurs* / Pier Paolo Tamburelli

This book collects sketches I made for eight lectures I gave at Vienna Technical University (TU Wien) in the 2021 winter semester. The lectures were part of the so-called *Grundkurs* or "basic course" that architecture students at the TU Wien take in the first semester of their first year. The course is meant as a first encounter with the discipline. Its fundamental question is nothing less than: "What is Architecture about?"

The *Grundkurs* was the first course I taught when I joined the faculty of the TU in September 2021. Although students still called it the *Grundkurs*, by that time it had changed its official designation to *Grundlagen des Entwerfens*: that is, "Foundations of Design," or maybe "Fundamentals of Design," if not "Basics of Design." In homage to the peculiar strain of Viennese madness known as "logical positivism," I've retained the old name here (for all its shortcomings, the jargon of logical positivism is better than the jargon of bureaucracy). *Grundkurs* indeed sounds very much like *Grundnorm* (the hypothetical rule that, according to Kelsen's *Pure Theory of Law*, provides the foundation of an entire legal system) and suggests a similar purity of intent in addressing Architecture with a capital A, and addressing it all at once. Loyalty to the *Grundkurs*—at least to its name—signals a sincere desire not to skirt around the question, not to avoid the naivety required to ask: "What is Architecture about?"

I suspect the *Grundkurs* was the brainchild of Rob Krier, who held the chair of "Gestaltungslehre und Entwerfen" before András Pálffy and me. And I suspect that much of the substantial supply of architectural primers Krier has produced over his lifetime is related to the *Grundkurs*. In a way the very undidactic nature of my *Grundkurs* is a reaction to that fascinatingly unbearable set of instructions on how to design square and circular pillars, square and circular houses, square and circular squares, square and circular cities. While I cannot subscribe to the idea of a wholesale theory of architecture, starting with pillars and ending with regional planning, I do admire Krier's courage and I have certainly been inspired by the narrative potential of his sketches. Probably also the deliberately ugly, punk tone of some of my drawings is a reaction to Krier's, although I shouldn't blame others for the way I draw, as I don't know how to do it any differently.

While I do not wish to avoid the question "What is Architecture about?" I must admit that I have no answer for it: I cannot provide a complete theory of architecture, and even less a brief, introductory version of it. As a consequence, my approach to the *Grundkurs* has been rather open-ended and deliberately non-exhaustive. The eight lessons simply list eight sets of alternatives that I believe expose some of the fundamental problems of contemporary architecture. Each lesson addresses a dialectic couple: Roof / Wall, Shelter / Memory, Design / Analysis, Language / Action, Architecture / City, Profession / Art, Figure / Ground, Eclecticism / Classicism. All the lessons are organized as presentations made of fifty slides—I used a standard PowerPoint format—with each slide composed as a diptych. The image on the left always refers to the first semantic area (so Roof, Shelter, Design…), while the image on the right always refers to the second one (Wall, Memory, Analysis…); a few slides include just one image. Some pictures resurface time and again in different contexts and with different meanings. Readers will notice that I tend to have a greater sympathy for the terms in the second column (for art more than profession, for ground more than figure, and so forth), but this preference never develops into a real "theory," neither is there an attempt at achieving much consistency (someone more committed to ground, for instance, should probably also prefer the profession to art, but…) The couples are "dialectical," so there is somehow a thesis and an antithesis but no hint at a synthesis, to deploy a vaguely Hegelian terminology for a moment. Long live the great Georg Wilhelm Friedrich, but the theoretical ambition here is not so high. That is why, for instance, "architecture" appears as one of the alternative terms that are supposed to explain architecture itself. This conceptual sloppiness is, to a certain extent, deliberate, for the *Grundkurs* is nothing more than an introduction, a clumsy sleepwalking in the direction of architecture. And this is also why this bunch of notes remains so proudly unsystematic and often succumbs to the temptation of the anecdote, unable to resist visual affinities, once again at the expenses of conceptual rigor.

This "prevalence of the visual" corresponds to two assumptions, one related to architecture as a discipline and the other related to a possible pedagogy of architecture at this particular moment in time. The first assumption is that architecture is a figurative art and that architecture's fundamental experiences are visual experiences. This means that the first thing to learn in architecture is how *to see*, to educate the eye, to learn how to look at buildings and to look at paintings in order to acquire that capacity for educated seeing that Michelangelo aptly described as "having the compass in the eyes" (*le seste negli occhi*). The second assumption is that, in an image-based society, students would probably be attracted and convinced more by the beauty of images than by the rigor of an argument. So, my idea for the *Grundkurs* is that, first of all, students should *see pictures*, should become familiar with a set of canonical works and then, on the basis of these images, could start addressing all the problems that are associated with them.

The list of topics addressed in the eight lessons is certainly not conclusive (and by the way I also prepared a few other lessons, for example on Private / Public and on Necessity / Representation, that were never presented to the students and consequently are not published here). The selection of topics simply outlines a possible approach to architecture and attempts to address the question "What is Architecture about?" by also asking "Why is Architecture relevant in our culture?" I tried to give the students an idea of architecture as cultural production—an idea of design as an intellectual operation—and to define a context in which to situate this practice. The lessons are built around confrontations between opposing design solutions to the rather limited range of intellectual problems that architecture can tackle. They try to show how these different formal configurations depend on (and expose) different world views, different values. They try to show why architecture matters, why we attribute meaning to it, why and how it is possible to detect a project for an entire civilization in the way Leonidov assembles an inverted cone and a sphere or in the manner the head of a horse is squeezed into the pediment of the Parthenon.

The images used for the lessons are either scans from books in my office or materials found through banal online searches. While preparing the lessons, I redrew all the images from the screen of my laptop: the point of the sketches was just to identify and memorize the images and to gain the time, while making them, to think about something to say. Next to these scribbles I put notes, drew arrows, copied quotes, added bibliographical references. These short texts are generally in English (a rather basic English), with occasional quotes in Italian or German. They are generally written in block capitals, to be easily read while lecturing. The notes are not meant as a structured essay—and this is also the reason why they are not transcribed in this book, which is, after all, a book of sketches, and not a draft of an accomplished theory. Sometimes the oppositions suggested in the notes are very crude (see for instance the brutal pairing of "column / hero, column / tragedy" with "wall / comedy, wall / community"). Some may sound silly, others are by now unfathomable to me as well, such as "Devil's Tower becomes architecture because it is precisely chosen by the aliens."

The drawings are not particularly nice. They are also not so architectural, and they are rather different from the ones I do while actually designing buildings. In fact, the design sketches I make in the office are even more casual: I draw with whatever pen on whatever paper comes to hand—usually the back of recycled sheets. In the case of the *Grundkurs* notes, the pen and the paper are always the same: a black marker, neither thick nor thin, and two notebooks with slightly more proper paper. This otherwise unrequired nicety became necessary in order to maintain the continuity in format and expose the narrative that runs through the different lessons. This continuity (together with the not entirely unintentional silliness of some drawings) ends up turning the drawings into a sort of comic strip. And I must admit that although I do not read many comics, and am definitely no comic nerd, I like them, and have even made comics (at school as a teenager and even more recently, but fortunately never dared to publish them).

Comics at least provide some relief from the unavoidable confrontation with the Italian tradition of teaching by means of sketches, as Carlo Aymonino and Enzo Mari did. Unlike Aymonino's drawings, mine are never *en plein air*, never from real life; they do not correspond to travels, to romances, to girlfriends; they were all made at the kitchen table in front of a PowerPoint presentation, when the kids were in bed or at least should have been. They are rather detached, conventional, and independent of personal life; they simply serve as examples to build up the alternatives highlighted in the lessons. The only similarity with Aymonino are a few long quotes from classical authors, dropped in here and there to fix a few anchoring points for the argument and simulate some sort of intellectual decency. And in contrast to Mari, my drawings are far less "designed." Mari's pages are incredibly composed: text is always impeccably readable and fills the space among figures in a perfectly balanced manner. He addresses the readers directly, burying them under a frozen lava of unremitting and yet perfectly composed, moralizing accusations. My drawings are far less committed and far less aggressive. Their tone is objective/cynical, sometimes sarcastic. Maybe in the end the *Grundkurs* simply tries to guess "What Architecture is not about."

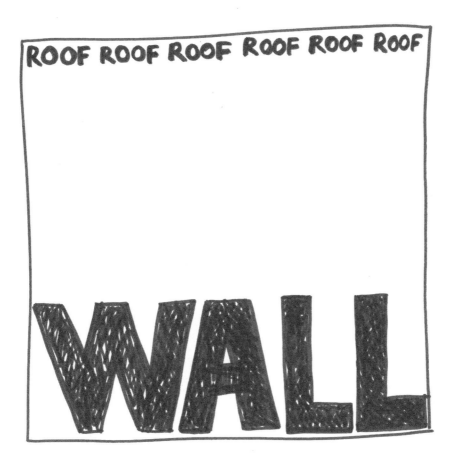

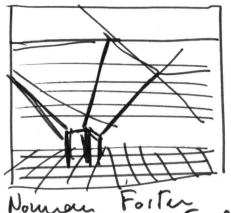

Norman Foster
Stansted Airport 1981

Piranesi - Foro
Augusto - 1757 ← per Piranesi
VEDUTE DI ROMA   Foro di Nerva

TECTORUM UTILITAS OMNIUM EST PRIMA ET MAXIMA
Alberti, De re aedificatoria 1, XI, p. 75 ed Portoghesi
1450 ca. / / / / / / / /

IMMER IST DIE RAUMSCHLIESSUNG DIESES SUBJEKTES
DIE ERSTE HAUPTANGELEGENHEIT, D.H. DIE EINFRIEDIGUN
ODER UMWANDUNG NACH DEN SEITEN ZU, NICHT DIE
BEDACHUNG NACH OBEN
Schmarsow, Das Wesen der architektonischen Schöpfu
1893

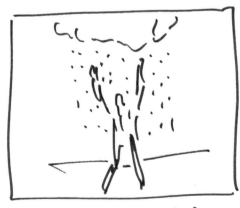

Filarete   1460
Magliabechiano

ROOF
PHYSICS
TECHNOLOGY
ENVELOPE

SUSPICIOUS
ABSENCE
OF
VIOLENCE

Hans Weiditz 1495-1537
Romulus Remus

VIOLENCE
AND
CRITIQUE
OF VIOLEN

THE CITY
ON THE
BACKGROUN
AS A
SILENT
POLITICA
SCENE

WAR
POLITICS
PRAXIS
SEPARATION

MA E' DA CREDERE CHE SUBITO ADAMO FU
CACCIATO DAL PARADISO ET PIOUENDO ET NON
AUENDO ALTRO PIÚ PRESTO RICOUERO, SI
MISSE LE MANI IN CAPO PER DIFENDERSI
DALL' ACQUA. ET SICHOME COSTRETTO DALLA
NECESSITA' PER VIVERE IL MANGIARE, COSÍ L'ABITARE
ERA MESTIERO PER DIFENDERSI DA MALI TEMPI
E DALL' ACQUE. ALLUNO DICE CHE ~~ADAMO~~
~~mmmmm~~ INNANZI A DILUUIO NON PIOUEUA,
O CREDO PIÚ DI SÍ, SE LA TERRA DOUEUA
PRODU~~XXX~~CERE I FRUTTI BISOGNAUA CHE
PIOUESSE

Filarete I, IV, 5

LIGHT / HEAVY
↓ ↓
FREE ← SMALL BIG ⟶ COLLECTIVE
(?) ↓ ↓
PRIVATE "ETERNAL"

Although ~~entirely private~~
architecture cannot be
entirely private

THIS IS A PROBLEM FOR
CONTEMPORARY ARCHITECTURE
AND A RESOURCE!

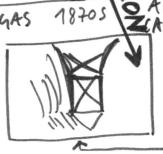

DEGAS 1870S

ANDREA DI BONAIUTO
CAPPELLONE SPAGNOLI 1365-70 ca.

GIEDEON

PIRANESI
ANTICHITÀ ROMANE 1756
FOUNDATIONS
THEATRE OF MARCELLUS

GALERIE
DES
MACHINES
1889

THIS THING
IS NOT LIGHT
IT JUST LOOKS

ABU SIMBEL REBUILT 1960-64

BEAUBOURG BUILT 1971-1977

⤷ IN THE MEANTIME MATTA-CLARCK
MARLO FERRERI "TOUCHE PAS À LA FEMME BLANCHE"

CONICAL INTERSECT 197

HEAVY AND LIGHT AS VISUAL CATEGORIES

INVERT

← HEAVY   LIGHT →

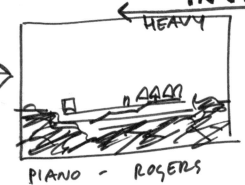

PIANO - ROGERS

MATTA CLARCK

THIS IS A MONUMENT AS WELL

ANTI-MONUMENTAL MONUMENT ?

WALL AS "ABSENCE OF WALL" AS CRITIQUE

THE WALL IS A TOOL IN AN ARCHITECTURE WHOSE SCOPE IS A <u>GESTURE</u>

⤷ Wittgens

ROOF AS MONUMENTAL ELEMENT

DORIC

PAESTUM

RAN

KUROSAWA - RAN 1985

WALL AS IMMATERIAL SEPARATION

DORIC!!!

ROOF   NEUE
NATIONALGALERIE
1962 - 68

SEIDE

LILLY   REICH
MVDR   1927
WOMEN'S FASHION
EXHIBITION

WALLS AS
PURE SEPARATION

CONSEQUENCE
OF AN ARCHITE
CTURE THAT
WANTED TO BE
WITHOUT WALLS

5 POINTS
· PILOTIS
· PLAN LIBRE
· FAÇADE LIBRE
· FENETRE   EN
   LONGEUR
· TOIT JARDIN

The problem of
the Doric Temple is
the construction of
the Doric Temple.
Doric architecture
is fundamentally
indifferent to
what happens inside
of it.
(Actually nothing
happens in Doric
Architecture)

ROOF   WALL

BARRAGAN
ROOF ALWAYS MEAN COLUMN

AS FIGURATIVE
ELEMENTS

WALL IS SOMEHOW
AN ABSOLUTE ELEMENT
AN ARCHITECTURE OF
WALLS ALONE   IS
POSSIBLE / NO ROOF
                ALONE

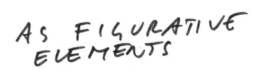

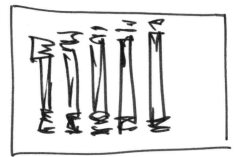

COLUMNS 5 ORDERS
Perrault

TECTONIC ELEMENTS
FOUNDED IN NATURAL
LAWS

└──→ conventions
as opposed to
nature ──→ Perrault ORDRE
FRANÇAIS

Vignola conventions
as foundational

LOOS
CHICAGO
TRIBUNE
1922
Column as
a precedent ──→

IS IT A JOKE?

OLD
ARCHITECTURE

COLUMN
AS A FRAGM
OF THE CIT
TO BE
RE-USED

(Column as
wall / as
icon at
the same tim

§ LA QUERELLE DES §
§ ANCIENS ET DES §
§ MODERNES §

NEW
ARCHITECTURE

William Chambers
1759 TREATISE ON
CIVIL ARCHITECTURE

BRAMANTE
CANONICA
S. AMBROGIO
1492 - 99

AGAIN -
A JOKE?

MANTEGNA 1481

ANTONELLO 1478

GHIRLANDAIO 1485-90
CAPPELLA TORNABUONI
SANTA MARIA NOVELLA

WALL AS A TOOL FOR

GESTURES TO APPEAR

GIOTTO
AND ALL
ITALIAN
RENAISSANCE

RELATION
PAINTING
ARCHITECTURE
BASED ON THE
WALL AS
SURFACE

WALL
AS OPERATOR
SEPARATING
THINGS
HAPPENING
INSIDE
AND
OUTSIDE

COLUMN AS ORNAMENT
IN AN ARCHITECTURE
UNDERSTOOD AS
COMPOSITION OF
VOLUMES

IN TOTA RE AEDIFICATORIA
PRIMARIUM CERTE ORNAMENTUM
IN COLUMNIS EST

Alberti VI, XIII

COLUMN / HERO
COLUMN / TRAGEDY

LA PICTURA NON
E' SE NON
DIMOSTRATIONI
DE SUPERFICIE

Piero, De prospectiva
pingendi

WALL / COMEDY
WALL / COMMUNITY

1971

"IT IS 165 KM LONG"

BERLIN WALL AS ARCHITECTURE

EXCLUSION AS ESSENTIAL ELEMENT OF ARCHITECTURE

HORROR / BEAUTY

ARCHIGRAM

SUPERSTUDIO

1972

For Koolhaas architecture is a means to an end

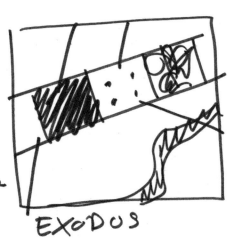

EXODUS

THE GOOD HALF

THE BAD HALF

THE WALL WAS A MASTERPE

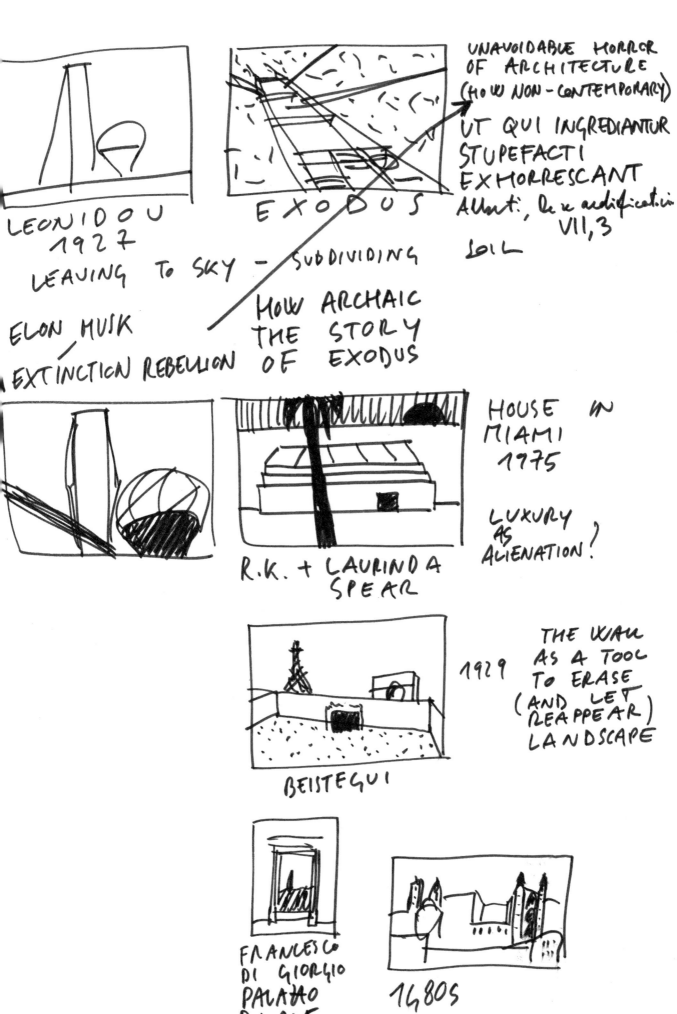

LEONIDOU
1927

EXODUS

UNAVOIDABLE HORROR
OF ARCHITECTURE
(HOW NON-CONTEMPORARY)

UT QUI INGREDIANTUR
STUPEFACTI
EXHORRESCANT
Alberti, De re aedificatoria
VII,3

LEAVING TO SKY — SUBDIVIDING   SOIL

ELON MUSK
EXTINCTION REBELLION

HOW ARCHAIC
THE STORY
OF EXODUS

HOUSE IN
MIAMI
1975

LUXURY
AS
ALIENATION?

R.K. + LAURINDA
SPEAR

1929   THE WALL
AS A TOOL
TO ERASE
(AND LET
REAPPEAR)
LANDSCAPE

BEISTEGUI

FRANCESCO
DI GIORGIO
PALAZZO
DUCALE

1480S

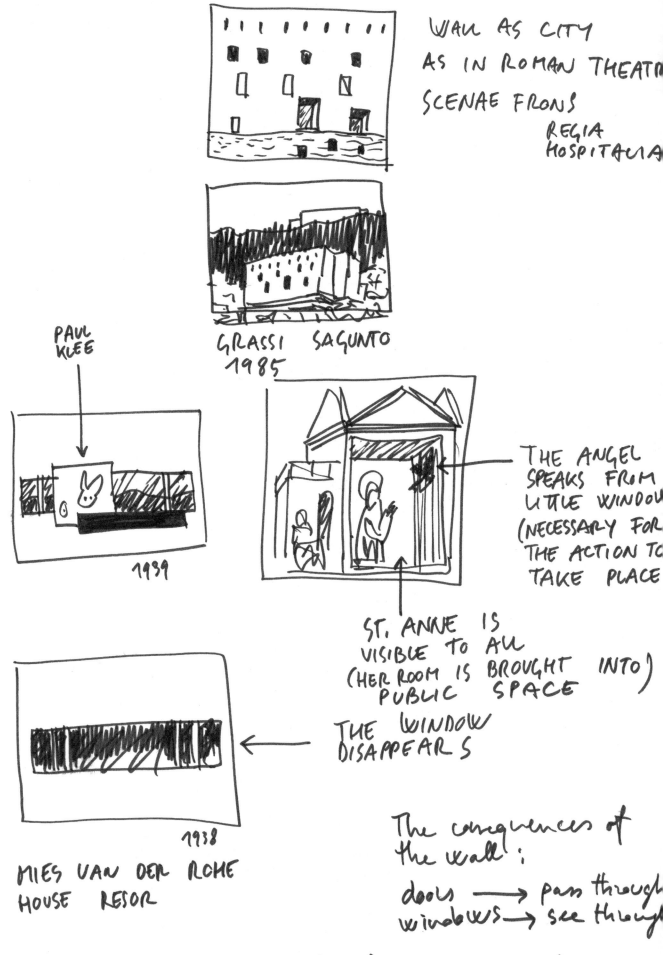

WALL AS CITY
AS IN ROMAN THEATR
SCENAE FRONS
REGIA
HOSPITALIA

PAUL
KLEE

GRASSI SAGUNTO
1985

1939

THE ANGEL
SPEAKS FROM
LITTLE WINDOW
(NECESSARY FOR
THE ACTION TO
TAKE PLACE

ST. ANNE IS
VISIBLE TO ALL
(HER ROOM IS BROUGHT INTO)
PUBLIC SPACE

THE WINDOW
DISAPPEARS

1938

MIES VAN DER ROHE
HOUSE RESOR

The consequences of
the wall:

doors ——→ pass through
windows ——→ see through

DOORS AND WINDOWS AS NON-WALL

SHINOHARA

STRUTH MILAN
CATHEDRAL

ROOF AND WALL CAN BECOME ELEMENTS
OF A "LANGUAGE"
THE SYMBOL IS MORE IMPORTANT THAN THE
PERFORMANCE   (A NON-ARCHITECTURAL APPROACH
                TO   ARCHITECTURE)

NEUE NATIONALGALERIE

PERGAMON

ROOF AS IMAGE   OF   A ROOF
DOOR AS IMAGE OF   A DOOR

ARCHITECTURE IS REPRESENTATION
        NOT NECESSAIRILY ONLY

GRASSI: OGGETTO E RAPPRESENTAZIONE
         DELLE NORME CHE LO GOVERNANO

G. Grani, Architecture dead language, Quaderni
         di Lotus, 9, Milano, 1988

    THE WALL IS   OPAQUE,
    SO IT SEPARATES INSIDE
    AND OUTSIDE

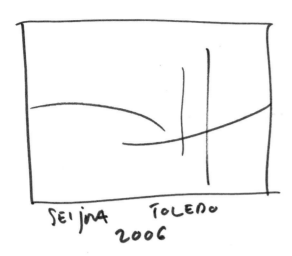

SEIJMA   TOLEDO
2006

ENFILADE
KUNSTHISTORISCHES
1871-91 GOTTFRIED SEMPER

TRANSPARENCY — SEPARATION

Colin Rowe, Robert Slutzky,
Transparency, literal and
Phenomenal", in "Perspecta", 8
1963, p. 45-54

WALL AS THE OPERATOR
OF A PRIVATE / PUBLIC
ALTERNATIVE

LL VILLA STEIN
1927-28

LOOS HAUS 1909

VILLE SAVOYE

LOOS APARTMENT
1903

B. Colomina, Privacy and Publicity, 1995

SECTION / PLAN

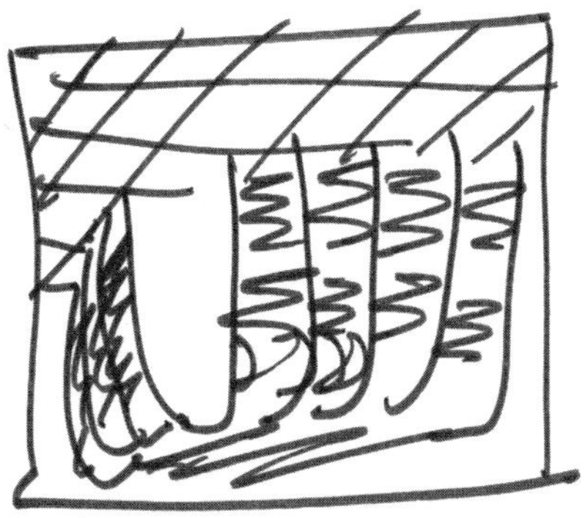

PIANO
PROMETEO
1984

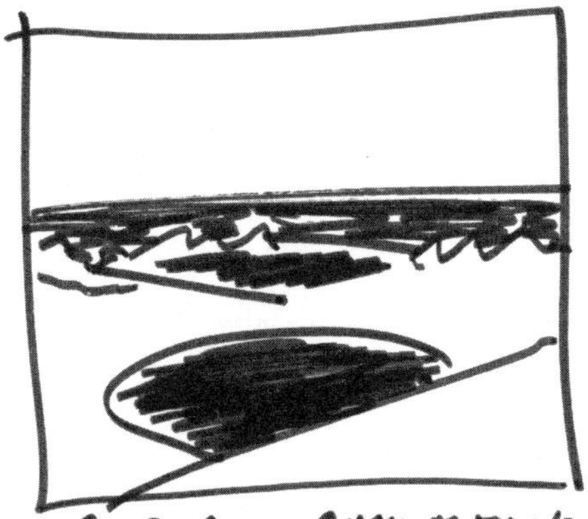

SIZA SWIMMING
POOL LECA DE
PALMEIRA 1966

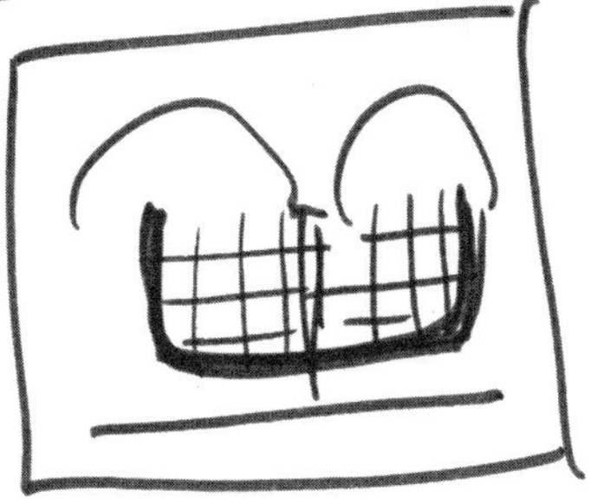

PIANO
PROMETEO

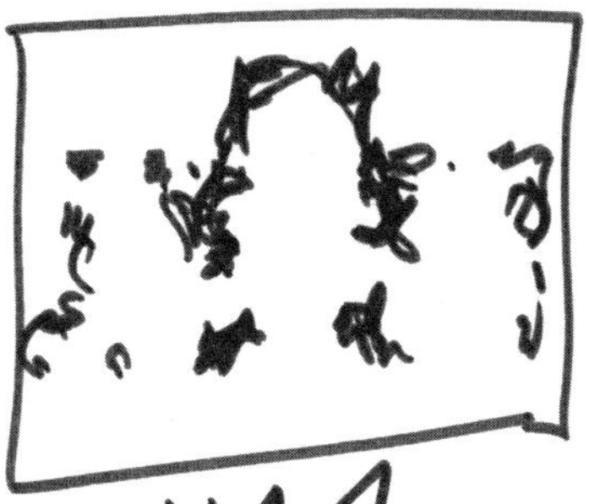

VA 1

DOMENICO FONTANA
DELLA TRASPORTATIONE
DELL'OBELISCO
VATICANO
1590

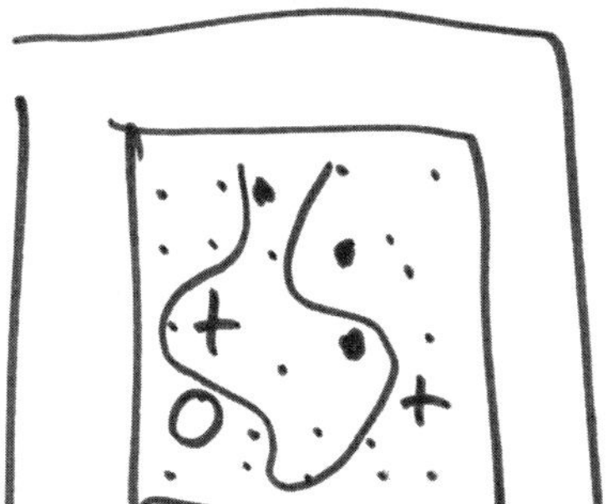

OMA AGADIR
1990

*Fontana solves at technical
level what Bramante could
only address at ~~its ideo~~ ideological
level

24

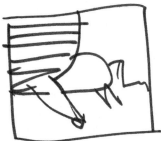

WALKING
CITY
ARCHIGRAM

Nolli map
1748

GEOLOGICAL
SECTION

MANHATTAN
GRID

(MANHATTAN IS
POSSIBLE
BECAUSE OF
ITS GEOLOGICAL
CONDITION)

ACROPOLIS

POINTS
IN LANDSCAPE
(UNTOUCHED)

DEIR EL BAHARI
REPEATED WALLS

W.F. OTTO, DIE GÖTTER GRIECHENLANDS
The appearance of the god
in the precise place
the lightning as a
spatial paradigm
Heraclitus "the lightning steers the universe"

DELPHI

IX - III century BCE

The visitor moves freely in space

LUXOR
1400 BCE
AMENOFI III

The subject does not turn in space. He just moves in space left and right

A series of walls to be looked at frontally

THE SPACE INVADERS LOGIC

MOVES ONLY LEFT/RIGHT →

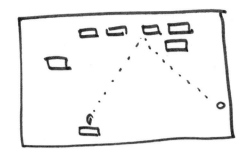

WALL AFTER
WALL AFTER
WALL

ALWAYS SAME
LOGIC

THE MORE YOU
PROGRESS THE
MORE SOCIALLY
EXCLUSIVE

more and more
inaccessible
text

WALL AND
DOOR

TEXT EVERYWHERE
THE EGYPTIAN TEMPLE AS
A COLOSSAL COMPUTER MEMORY
AS A DATA CENTRE

DETAILS ONLY
AT VERY FEW
PLACES

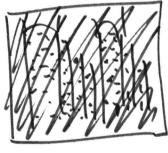

DETAILS EVERYWHERE
INFORMATION EVERYWHERE

PARTHENON
HORSE HEAD

ARCHITECTURE
AS SCULPTURE

ARCHITECTURE
AS GRAPHIC
DESIGN

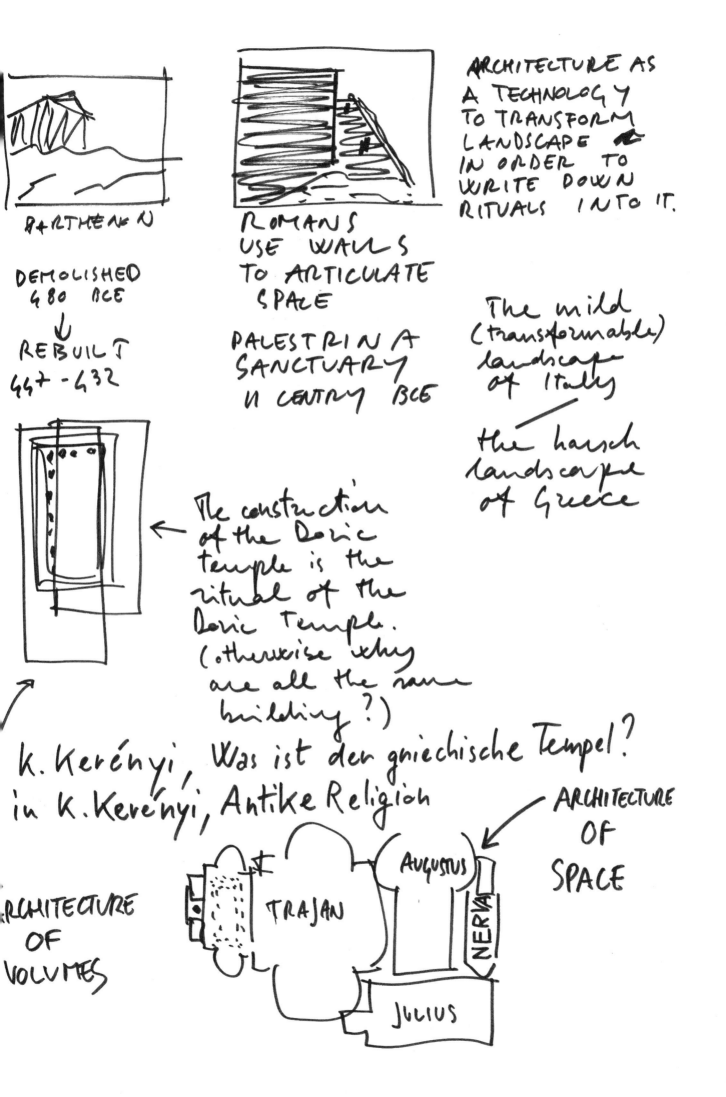

PARTHENON

DEMOLISHED
480 BCE
↓
REBUILT
447 - 432

ROMANS
USE WALLS
TO ARTICULATE
SPACE

PALESTRINA
SANCTUARY
II CENTURY BCE

ARCHITECTURE AS
A TECHNOLOGY
TO TRANSFORM
LANDSCAPE
IN ORDER TO
WRITE DOWN
RITUALS INTO IT.

The mild
(transformable)
landscape
of Italy

the harsch
landscape
of Greece

← The construction
of the Doric
temple is the
ritual of the
Doric Temple.
(otherwise why
are all the same
building?)

K. Kerényi, Was ist der griechische Tempel?
in K. Kerényi, Antike Religion

ARCHITECTURE
OF
VOLUMES

TRAJAN

AUGUSTUS

NERVA

JULIUS

ARCHITECTURE
OF
SPACE

CHOISY — ACROPOLIS

Histoire de l'architecture
1899

The subject moves
attracted by POINTS

The subject
flows inside
of pre-established
channels

RAFFAELLO
SCUOLA DI ATENE

The movement under
the barrel vault
the barrel vault as
the equivalent of that
movement

AN ARCHITECTURE
OF VOIDS

VOLUMES ARE

"des elements
en soi amorphe
et sans
individualité

METTERNICH
Le PREMIER
PROJET POUR
St. PIERRE DE
ROME 1975

BRAMANTE
SANTA MARIA
DELLE GRAZIE
1492 99

TEMPLE A

GREECE
ROME
ALTERNATIVE
ACCORDING TO
ADOLF LOOS
ARCHITEKTUR 1910

"IT IS NOT MERE CHANCE
THAT ROMANS WERE
INCAPABLE OF INVENTING A NEW ORDER...

LOOS 1912 "

SHELTER

MEMORY

THE SHELTER / MEMORY ALTERNATIVE
IS FUNDAMENTALLY THE SAME ROOF/WAL
ALTERNATIVE, JUST LOOKING AT THE
SCOPE INSTEAD THAN LOOKING AT THE
TOOL

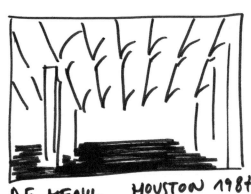

DE MENIL   HOUSTON 1987
RENZ   PIANO

MASSO DEI
METELLI

MEMORY   THROUGH
IMAGES

MEMORY   THROUGH
RITUALS

WHAT DOES ARCHITECTURE DO ?

DEFINES AN
ENVIRONMENT
FOR A   RECENT VERSION
OF THIS   APPROACH SEE
P. RAHM, NATURAL HISTORY
OF ARCHITECTURE

COUPLES BEHAVIOUR
WITH PLACES
DISTRIBUTES RESOURCE

REPRESENT THESE
BEHAVIOURS AND THESE
DISTRIBUTION

A DETERMINIST
READING OF
THE HISTORY
OF THE CITY
CITIES CHANGE
BECAUSE OF EPIDEMICS
AND OTHER AMENITIES

KEEP OUR BODY TEMPERATURE
AT 37° C

ARCHITECTURE AS
CLOTHING (AS INSULATION)

ARCHITECTURE
AS (REPRESENTED)
POLITICS

ARCHITECTURE STARTS FROM THE HOUSE / ARCHITECTURE STARTS FROM THE TEM

ALEPPO CITADEL

PISA CEMETERY

P.P. PASOLINI
MEDEA
1969

CITY WALLS/FORTRESSES
AS ARCHITECTURE OF
SHELTER THAT BECOMES
SYMBOLIC

OF UNITY!
OF PROTECTION?
OF FEAR?

THIS IS THE MOMENT
A RADICALLY NEW
PARADIGM APPEARS

ARCHITECTURE
AS DISTANCE
AMONG DIFFERENT
ACTIONS TO BE
PER FORMED

ARCHITECTURE
AS CONTROL OF
TIME ATTRIBUTED
TO GESTURES

PRECISION

CLARITY

The acropolis of Corinth is made of exterior of Aleppo Citadel + interior Pisa cemetery

ARCHITECTURE
AS MONTAGE
Bramante
Le Corbusier
Stirling

LAUGIER
ESSAI 1753

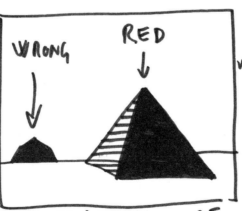

WRONG   RED

TWO PYRAMIDS OF
SNOFRU IN DASHUR
(THE WRONG AND RED ONE)

from
GIEDION
"The Eternal
Past" 1962

see
late
LC

A CRITIQUE OF
MODERNISM THAT
DOES NOT GO BACK TO

CLASSICISM

Rousseau's Discours sur l'origine et les fondaments
de l'inégalité parmi les hommes 1755

A. Smith, Wealth of Nations 1776

D. Hume, Enquiry concerning Human understanding
1748

TWO YEARS
AFTER!

VILLA STEIN 1928

See against late le Corbusier
G.C. Argan, la chiesa di Ronchamp, 1956, in "Progetto e destino"

CHANDIGARM ASSEMBLY 1959 - 1962

AN ARCHITECT OF MEMORY BUILT WITH MODERNIST TOOL BOX

→ baroque
→ mixture of architectural and religious function

the point is indeed the use of architecture as a technology of memory

MAN (ALONE)
↓
NEEDS
↓
ARCHITECTURE

SUBDIVISION RITUAL ANIMAL
↗
SUBDIVISION CITY

LUNDA XVII - XIX century

the image is maybe from Rudowsky "Architecture without Architects" BUT I DON'T KNOW

WHILE, IN THIS CONTEXT, "SHELTER" IS ALWAYS
NDIVIDUAL, "MEMORY" IS ALWAYS THE MEMORY
F A COMMUNITY

N. De Moncheaux
SPACESUIT, FASHIONING
APOLLO, MIT PRESS, 2011

CLOSE ENCOUNTERS
OF THE THIRD KIND
(S. Spielberg, 1977)

RICHARD
DREYFUSS

ALIENS WILL LAND AT
DEVIL'S TOWER AND
COMMUNICATE THE
IMAGE TO THE
SELECTED PEOPLE

ARCHITECTURE AS THE
LINK AMONG A PLACE
AND A BEHAVIOUR, AN
ACTION, A MEANING
(WITHOUT THE NEED
OF BUILT INTERVENTIONS)

DEVIL'S TOWER BECOMES
ARCHITECTURE BECAUSE
IT IS PRECISELY CHOSEN
BY THE ALIENS

IS THIS
ARCHITECTURE?
AND, IF SO, WHY?

AN ENVIRONMENT
ENTIRELY DEFINED
BY ARCHITECTURE

GERHARD RICHTER
NIAGARA FALLS
1965

THE TRANSFORMATION
OF LANDSCAPE
ARCHITECTURE AS
CULTURAL APPROPRIATION

V. Gregotti, Il territorio
dell'architettura, Milano
1966

SAME WAY TO DEPICT NATURE
WITH NO INTEREST IN NATURE

ARCHITECTURE AS
CLOTHING

Fischer von Erlach 1721
CATERACTES DU NIL

WATERFALLS AS THE PLACE
WHERE A MYTHICAL INTERPRETATION
IS ASSOCIATED TO A PLACE

ARCHITECTURE
AS MARKING

STRANGELY SIMILAR RESULTS

SPACE TECH
AS BRICOLAGE

HAGIA SOPHIA
AS MERZBAU

SCHWITTERS
MERZBAU 1933

MERZ BAU
A CONSTRUCTION OF
MEMORY, TOWARDS
INSIDE?
JUST A PRIVATE
MEMORY?
FRAGMENTS AS
INNER FRAGMENTS?
THE MERZBAU AS
A PUBLIC INTERIOR?

MEMORY AS SYMBOL
AS ICON

...TUR 1933

RODUCE
CONDITION

EPRESENT
CONDITION

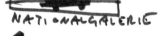

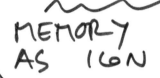
NATIONALGALERIE

MOUNT
RUSHMORE,
LINCOLN

LOOS
CHICAGO
TRIBUNE

ROSSI
SEGRATE
1965

SORT OF
SCULPTURE

ARCHIGRAM
RCHITECTURE AS
NEW WAY OF LIFE

IF SCULPTURE IS BIG ENOUGH
IT BECOMES ARCHITECTURE

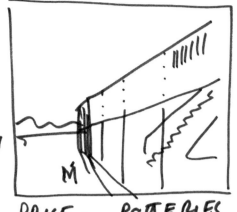

PRICE. POTTERIES
THINK BELT 1966

HITCHCOCK NORTH
BY NORTH WEST
1959

HOW DOES ARCHITECTURE (OF ALL SORTS)
BECOME SCENE? LANDSCAPE?

WHILE IT PROVIDES
AN AMBIENT, IT
PROVIDES A'N
ATMOSPHERE

WHILE IT PRODUCES
FIGURES, IT DEFINES
A SCENE WHERE ACTIONS
TAKE PLACE

THESE
BUBBLES
ARE
CALLED
"BIOMES"

The idea of a
complete control
of the environment.
(and in the name
of nature)

GRIMSHAW - EDEN PROJECT

OPENED
2001

"INSPIRED BY NATURE"
(WHILE IT IS CLEARLY INSPIRED)
BY BUCKMINSTER FULLER

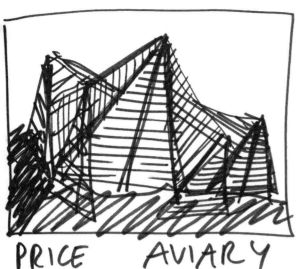

PRICE AVIARY
1963

THE AVIARY AS AN
ENVIRONMENT, AS A
NEW WORLD

is it
ARCHITECTURE
IF IT IS
NOT
ADDRESSED
TO
HUMANS?

LUBETKIN PENGUIN
POOL
1934

QUOTES EL LISSITZKY
MEYERHOLD THEATRE 1929
(FOR TAFURI IT PROVES THAT)
MODERN ARCHITECTURE WAS
ALREDY   DEAD

There is certainly
an element of farce
HIGHPOINT n CARYATIS

PENGUINS MUST MOVE ACCORDING
TO A SCRIPT

THIS TWO
REAPPEAR
IN EXCTLY
OPPOSITE
RELATION
IF WE CONSIDER
NOW SHELTER
/ MEMORY

RAN

AN ENVIRONMENT
SIMPLY MADE
OF WALLS

(IS THIS REALLY)
AN ENVIRONMENT?

PAESTUM

THE CONSTRUCTION
OF MEMORY BY
USING THE REPRESENTATION
OF SHELTER AS A
SYMBOL

OKTOBER FEST
BIER ZELT

TEMPORARY BUT NOT
SIMPLY PROVIDING SHELTER

PUBLIC BUT DESERTE

KARNAK

MEMORY AS DEPOSITED
(WRITTEN) IN STONE.
Jan Assman, Religion und
Kulturelles Gedächtnis, 200C

THE CONSTRUCTION OF COLLECT
MEMORY THROUGH "FIGURES
OF MEMORY" FOR INSTANCE
MONUMENTS (ANCIENT EGYPT)
AND BOOKS (ISRAEL)
            TEXT BECOMES UNCHANG
            ABLE (AND COMMENTARIE
                        BEGIN

DEREK JARMAN
GARDEN DUNGENESS
          1986 - 1994
GARDEN AS A COLLECTION
OF LIVING THINGS THAT
MIGHT EVOLVE ONE
NEXT TO THE OTHER

GARDENING AS
SHELTERING THESE
BEINGS

DEIR EL BAHARI,
QUEEN HATSHEPSUT
XVIII DINASTY

LANDSCAPE AS PURE
BACKGROUND FOR A
PURELY ARTIFICIAL
RECORDING OF CULTURAL
MEMORY

THE IMPOSSIBILITY
TO MAKE A CLEAR
PICTURE OF THE
JARMAN GARDEN

THE INCREDIBLE
CLARITY AND SIMPLICITY
OF THIS APPROACH
TO ARCHITECTURE AND
LANDSCAPE.
WRITING ON TERRITORY

THE EQUILIBRIUM
IS CONSTANTLY
CHANGING

EVERYTHING
IS FIXED

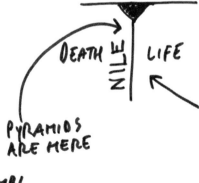

THE RELATION TO LANDSCAPE IS
INCREDIBLY DRY BUT NOT
UNREFINED
ALWAYS SAME EAST/WEST
GEOGRAPHIC/COSMIC/THEOLOGIC
ALTERNATIVE

ALL LANDSCAPE
IS ORGANIZED
PERPENDICULAR
TO THE NILE

DEATH | NILE | LIFE

PYRAMIDS
ARE HERE

NO PYRAMIDS
ON THE EASTERN
SIDE

THOMBI

PERPENDICULAR   PATHS
ORTHOGONAL   TO THE
NILE

EVERYTHING MUST
(FOR EVER) BE AT ITS
PLACE IN COSMOS, IN LAND,
IN SOCIETY. ALMOST 3000
YEARS OF NO CHANGE

ARCHITECTURE
AS A TOOL OF
ALTERING LAND-
SCAPE TO
IMPOSE AN
INTERPRETATION
IN EGYPT THIS
OPERATION REMAINS
AT AN INCREDIBLY
SIMPLE LEVEL

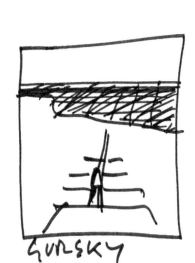

GURSKY

IV DINASTY
2600-2500 BCE

NILE

ROCK
~~EGYPT~~
PLATFORM

AGRICULTURAL
GRID

DESERT   AGRI

PYRAMIDS ARE IN
THE DESERT. THEY
DO NOT WASTE
CULTIVABLE LAND

PALESTRINA
(BAS PRINZEN 2014)

G. GULLINI, F. FASOLO IL SANTUARIO
DELLA FORTUNA PRIMIGENIA A
PALESTRINA, ROMA, 1953

PALADIO'S
INTERPRETATION
IS WRONG:
THE SANCTUARY
DOES NOT EXPOSE
ITS ORGANIZATION
IT SIMPLY _IMPOSES_
IT

PALESTRINA   MODEL
II CENTERY   BCE
BEFORE   TABULARIUM   78 BCE
SO FIRST COMPLETE
EXPRESSION OF ROMAN
ARCHITECTURE

- THE POSSIBILITY TO
  MODIFY CENTRAL ITALIAN
  LANDSCAPE (CONTRARY TO GREECE)
- THE TRANSFORMATION
  IS SITE-SPECIFIC AND
  CHANGES WITH DIFFERENT
  CONTEXTS (CONTRARY TO EGYPT)
- ARCHITECTURE AS
  COREOGRAPHY, AS A WAY
  TO USE OBSTACLES (WALLS)
  TO IMPOSE MOVEMENTS
- ARCHITECTURE AS A
  DEVICE TO DISCIPLINE
  CROWDS (BUT CONSIDER
  LIMITS OF THIS)
  ↳ FOUCAULT

SUPERSTUDIO
ARCHITECTURE AS
LIBERATING DEVICE (?)
FOR A FUTURISTIC
ARCADIA

- MARINA TOWERS
BERTRAND GOLDBERG 1959-64

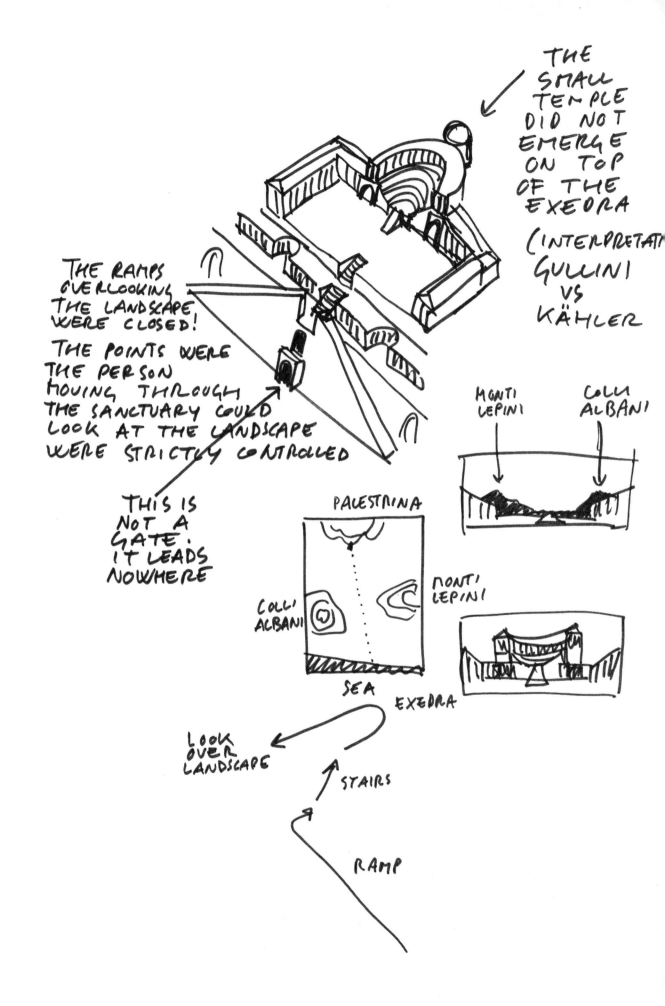

THE SMALL TEMPLE DID NOT EMERGE ON TOP OF THE EXEDRA

(INTERPRETATI GULLINI VS KÄHLER

THE RAMPS OVERLOOKING THE LANDSCAPE WERE CLOSED!

THE POINTS WERE THE PERSON MOVING THROUGH THE SANCTUARY COULD LOOK AT THE LANDSCAPE WERE STRICTLY CONTROLLED

THIS IS NOT A GATE. IT LEADS NOWHERE

MONTI LEPINI

COLLI ALBANI

PALESTRINA

COLLI ALBANI

MONTI LEPINI

SEA

EXEDRA

LOOK OVER LANDSCAPE

STAIRS

RAMP

THE ROMAN CALENDAR
AS A SERIES OF PRECISE
RITUALS TO BE PERFORMED
AT PRECISE PLACES

PULLARIUS

ARCHIZOOM
1971
"VESTIRSI È FACILE"

↓

EASINESS
RELAX
INFORMALITY

SEE MACHIAVELLI, DISCORSI
I, 14

ARCHITECTURE AS A
TECHNOLOGY OF THE
REPETITION (PRECISE
REPETITION) OF THESE
RITUAL ACTIONS AT
THESE PRECISE PLACES

ALDO SCHIAVONE, THE INVENTION
OF LAW IN THE WEST,
CAMBRIDGE, 2012

THE INVENTION OF
ARCHITECTURE ?

SEE
PLUTARCH, LIFE
OF NUMA (LIVES
OF LYCURGUS AND
NUMA - PARALLEL
LIVES)
The negotiation
among Numa and
(chapter 15) Jupiter
the literality of
Numa's interpretation

LOOS ⟶ STILL DO
ROMAN
ARCHITECTURE ?

ROMAN CALENDAR

FROM
D.
SABBATUCCI,
LA RELIGIONE
DI ROMA
ANTICA

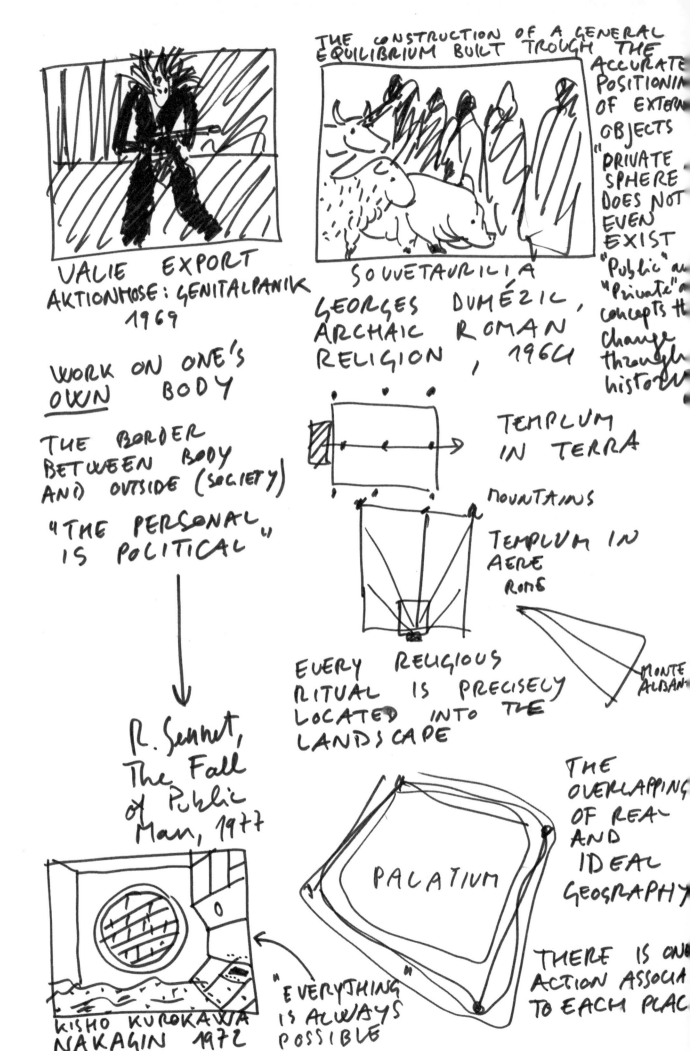

VALIE EXPORT
AKTIONHOSE: GENITALPANIK
1969

SOUVETAURILIA
GEORGES DUMÉZIL,
ARCHAIC ROMAN
RELIGION, 1964

THE CONSTRUCTION OF A GENERAL
EQUILIBRIUM BUILT TROUGH THE
ACCURATE
POSITIONI
OF EXTER
OBJECTS

"PRIVATE"
SPHERE
DOES NOT
EVEN
EXIST
"Public" a
"Private" a
concepts t
change
through
history

WORK ON ONE'S
OWN BODY

THE BORDER
BETWEEN BODY
AND OUTSIDE (SOCIETY)

"THE PERSONAL
IS POLITICAL"

TEMPLUM
IN TERRA

MOUNTAINS

TEMPLUM IN
AERE
RONS

EVERY RELIGIOUS
RITUAL IS PRECISELY
LOCATED INTO THE
LANDSCAPE

MONTE
ALBAN

R. Sennet,
The Fall
of Public
Man, 1977

PALATIUM

THE
OVERLAPPING
OF REAL
AND
IDEAL
GEOGRAPHY

THERE IS ON
ACTION ASSOCIA
TO EACH PLAC

KISHO KUROKAWA
NAKAGIN 1972

"EVERYTHING
IS ALWAYS
POSSIBLE"

THE TOPOGRAPHY
SURVIVES IN ROME
OF III CENTURY CE

1,5 MILLION
INHABITANTS

MODELLO
GISMONDI
1935-71
SCALE
1:250

PLAN

FORUM

CIRCUS MAXIMUS

PIRANESI READS
ALL THE FUTURE
OF ROME IN ITS
TOPOGRAPHY

FOUNDATION AS
THE FUNDUMENTAL
ACT OF
ARCHITECTURE

WALTER PICHLER
PROTOTYP 3 - 1966

48

PICHLER
PROTOTYP
1967

GIOVANNA   SILVA
CIRLO MASSIMO

23·03·2002   3M PEOPLE (?)
15·02·2003   "
ANTIQUITY   300.000

PIACENTINI
CITY HALL

1970S

RIVERS
SURVIVES
TURNED
INTO
STREETS

VALE DO
ANHANGABAÚ
SÃO PAULO

SAME RE-WRITIN
OF ORIGINAL
LANDSCAPE
AS IN ANCIEN
ROME

1878

1927

CAPE CANAVERAL
1950
VEHICLE ASSEMBLY
BUILDING
3,665,000 m³

BECOMES MONUMENT
BECAUSE OF SHEER SIZE
(ARCHITECTURE CAN BE RED ALSO AS PURE INVESTITM

BLACK STONE
OBJECT

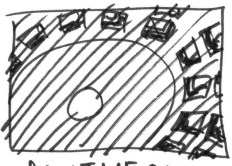

PANTHEON
VOID

KAADA
SHELTER FOR
BLACK STONE
KISWAH

ELEMENT IN THE
PERFORMANCE OF A
RITUAL.
TAWAF (CIRCLING THE
KAABA SEVEN TIMES
COUNTERCLOCKWISE)
6 M PILGRIMS/YEAR

DESIGN
_____
ANALYSIS

52

DES YEUX QUI
NE VOIENT PAS

LES PAQUEBOTS

VERS UNE
ARCHITECTURE
1923

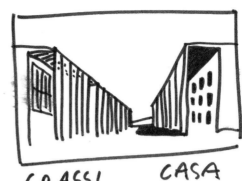

GRASSI   CASA
DELLO STUDENTE
CHIETI   1976-79

An object outside architecture
as the origin, the source
of a new architectural
production

AN IMMEDIATE, AUTHENTIC
LINK WITH THE SOURCE
OF INSPIRATION

"Noi diciamo che non c'è frattura
tra il momento dell'analisi e
quello del progetto, perché l'oggetto
dell'analisi è, in senso stretto,
lo stesso oggetto del progetto."

G. Grassi
ANALISI E PROGETTO
1969

← a critique of
Le Corbusier in
G. GRASSI, LA COSTR
ZIONE LOGICA DELL
ARCHITETTURA, 1967

Grassi exposes
link Laugier

↓

L.C.

Fischli and
Weiss

THE RELATION OF
ABSOLUTE PAST
AND ABSOLUTE PRESENT

PAESTUM

←— IT LOOKS SO OLD NOW

CAR 1907

PARTHENON

CAR 1921

L.C. 1923

PARTHENON

L.C. 1923

GRASSI'S CRITIQUE OF L.C.
AND LAUGIER IN "COSTRUZIONE
LOGICA"
THE OPERATION IS THE
SAME: THE REFERENCE TO
AN ABSOLUTE (AND ABSOLUTELY
PURE) ORIGIN JUSTIFIES AN
ABSOLUTELY NEW ARCHITECTURE.
NO SPACE FOR ELABORATION
IS LEFT IN BETWEEN

G. Grassi La costruzione
logica

R. Carnap Der logische
Aufbau der
Welt
(actually more H. Kelsen
Reine Rechtslehre)
1934

LAUGIER 1753

NATURE
↓
FREEDOM
(Rousseau,
Thoreau,
Romantics)

THE FIRST, PRIMITIVE HUT IS IRRELEVANT.
IT MATTERS ONLY AS THE OCCASION
FOR REFLECTING ON IT.
FOR ~~AN~~ ARCHITECTURE THE FIRST HUT
IS THE SECOND ONE

CONVENTION ———→ FREEDOM

PHILIPPE STARCK 1989
ASAHI SUPER DRY HALL

A CREATIVE ORIGINAL
GESTURE, SELF EVIDENT
DIRECTLY ROOTED IN
LIFE

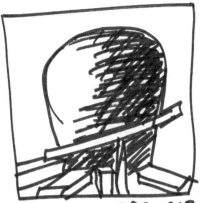

OMA. ZEEBRUGGE
SEA TERMINAL 1989

LEONIDOU LENIN
INSTITUTE + DALÍ
CRUTCHES

WHAT IS A CATHEDRAL? WHAT IS
A THEATRE? AN ATMOSPHERE? A SET
OF
EXAMPL?

K.F. SCHINKEL 1813
GOTISCHER DOM AM
WASSER
THERE ARE SEVERAL
COPIES OF THE PAINTING
UNTIL THE END OF
NAPOLEONIC WARS
FUNDAMENTALLY
JUST A (BAD) PAINTER

THE GOTHICNESS
OF THE GOTHIC
CATHEDRAL

THE TWO PHASES
OF SCHINKEL'S CAREER
THE DIFFERENCE AMONG
BEFREIUNGSDOM AND
FRIEDRICHSWERDERSCHE

DURAND PRECIS
DE LEÇONS D'ARCHITECTURE
1802 - 05
RECUEIL ET PARALLÈLE
DES ÉDIFICES DE TOUT GENR
ANCIENS ET MODERNES

1800

ARCHITECTURE OF THE PAST
AS A COLLECTION OF PRECEDEN
(PRECIS LOSES THE RICHNESS
OF THE EXEMPLES AND
BECOMES MORE OF A VERY
DRY METHOD)
INFLUENCE OF DURAND IN
SCHINKEL
ROMANTIC SCHINKEL/ CLASSICAL
SCHINKEL

FRIEDRICH WEINBRENNER
LANGE STRASSE KARLSRUHE
1806

GIORGIO GRASSI
1976 - 79

A VERY
PARTICULAR
FORM OF
ECLECTISM

HEINRICH TESSENOW
LANDESSCHULE
KLOTZSCHE 1925-27

GRASSI MODEL
CHIETI

GRASSI RE-DOES ~~THE SCHOOL~~
TESSENOW'S SCHOOL AND RE-DOES
WEINBRENNER'S STREET

ARCHITECTURE AS THE
ONLY WAY TO UNDERSTAND
ARCHITECTURE

1978

1987

AS GRASSI, THE BIG BLACK, IN
AN IDEAL HISTORY OF FORMS,
PUT THEMSELVES BEFORE THE
VERY SONG THEY ARE COVERING.
ANALYSIS DISCOVERS SOMETHING
MORE ESSENTIAL THAN THE
ORIGINAL ITSELF.
AUTHENTICITY IS DISMISSED AS
A ROMANTIC SUPERSTITION

SCHINKEL MAUSOLEUM
QUEEN LUISE 1810

CESARIANO
VITRUVIO 1527

GOTHIC AS
FEELING

THE YOUNG QUEEN
IS DEAD

GOTHIC AS
BUILDING TECHNIQUE

↓

ENTIRELY UNDERSTANDABLE
FROM A CLASSICIST POINT
OF VIEW

LOOKS
LIKE THE
COVER ART
FOR LED
ZEPPELIN
SINGLE

BRAMANTI OPINIO SUPER
DOMICILIUM SEU TEMPLUM MAGNU
1490

Bramante is entirely
indifferent to gothic
ornaments (he suggests to
copy them, as he would
do with those of the
Pantheon for St. Peter's

- Fortezza
- Conformità con el resto
  del edificio
- leggerezza
- bellezza

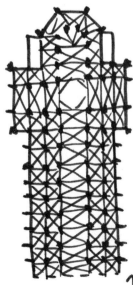

1386

J. Ackerman, The
Belvedere as a
classical villa,
Journal of the Warburg
and Courtland Institutes
14, 1951, p. 70-91

BERNARDO DELLA
VOLPAIA. CODEX CONER
FOL. 17V

BELVEDERE TOOLBOX

⬇

ALL OF BAROQUE
ROME

P. Letarouilly Le Vatican

SAME
SOLUTION
OF BASILICA
LEPTIS   VILLA
MAGNA   INNOCENIO
(BRAMANTE   VIII
NEVER SAW IT)

PANTHEON
+
BASILICA
MAXENTIUS

SERLIO
ST. PETER'S
DOME

QUOTE S. LORENZO

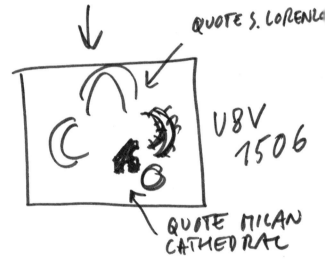

U8V
1506

QUOTE MILAN
CATHEDRAL

CORRECTIONS
BY BRAMANTE
OF GIULIANO
DA SANGALLO
U8R
ON THE BACK
OF THE SAME
PAPER

A PURELY
CRITICAL
ARCHITECTURE
"Angeborener
Kritischen
Verstand"

F. Wolff Metternich
BRAMANTE, SKIZZE EINES
LEBENSBILD, "BRAMANTE UND
ST. PETER", MÜNCHEN, 1975

PERUZZI UA2

REDENTORE 1577

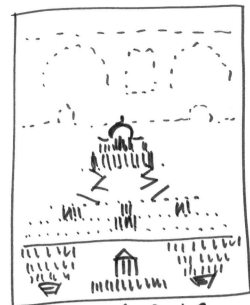

PALLADIO
INTERPRETATION
PALESTRINA

FOR PALLADIO THERE
IS A PAVILION AT EVERY
SINGLE CHANGE OF
DIRECTION.
ARCHITECTURE NEEDS
TO BE EXPLAINED
BEFORE BEING
PERFORMED

PHYSICAL
MUSCULAR
THE ~~MUSCULAR~~
RELATION TO
THE MOUNTAIN

Analysis
is limited
to relation
to landscape

PIETRO DA CORTONA a.1636

SANTI MARTINA E LUCA

PALESTRINA

THE
EMPTINESS
THERE

PARTICULARLY
IN THE DRY
SUMMER

CAPRAROLA
VIGNOLA   1560-73

AS CRUEL
AS PALESTRINA

THE BUILDING 14 CAN BE
DIVIDED INTO RECOGNIZABLE
PIECES THAT ARE PERFECTLY
JOINTED, BUT DO NOT MELT.

THE MONTAGE
OF DIFFERENT
UNRELATED
PIECES
THE RULE IS
NOT EXPOSED

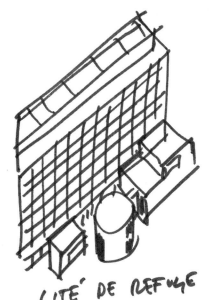

PALACE OF
SOVIETS

FORUM POMPEI

L. C.

CITÉ DE REFUGE
1933

THE WALL AS
A BACKGROUND
FOR MEASURING
OBJECTS IN FRONT
OF IT

WALL HOUSE II   1973

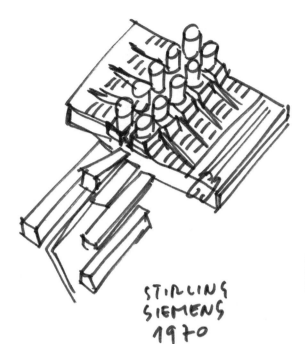

STIRLING
SIEMENS
1970

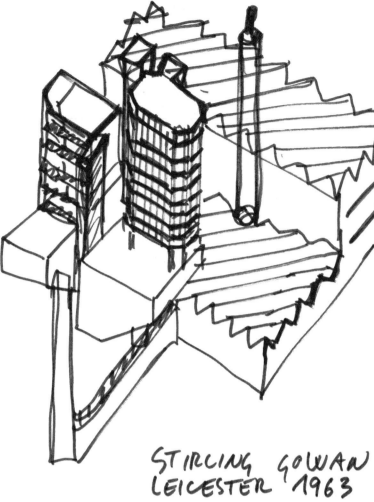

STIRLING GOWAN
LEICESTER 1963

THE PIECES ARE ALL
RECOGNIZABLE, MELNIKOV,
INDUSTRIAL ARCHITECTURE
THE LAW GOVERNING
THE ASSEMBLAGE CAN
BE DEDUCTED AND
BECOMES A PRECEDENT

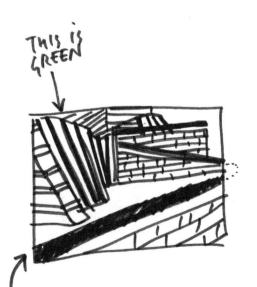

THIS IS
GREEN

THIS IS PINK
NEUE STAATSGALERIE
STUTGART 1984

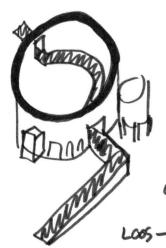

THE
ARCHITECTURAL
"DEVICE"
CAN BE
ENUCLEATED

↓

SEE BRAMANT
"OPINIO"

↓

LOOS → GOOD BUILDIN
CAN BE DESCRI

ONLY ARCHITECTURE IS DRAWN.
EVERYTHING THAT DEFINES
SPACE OR MODIFIES THE
PERCEPTION OF SPACE
(THE STEPS, THE DOORS, THE
WINDOWS)
NO STRUCTURE, NO INSULATION
THE <u>ABSTRACTION</u> OF
THESE <u>ANECDOTICAL</u> DRAWINGS

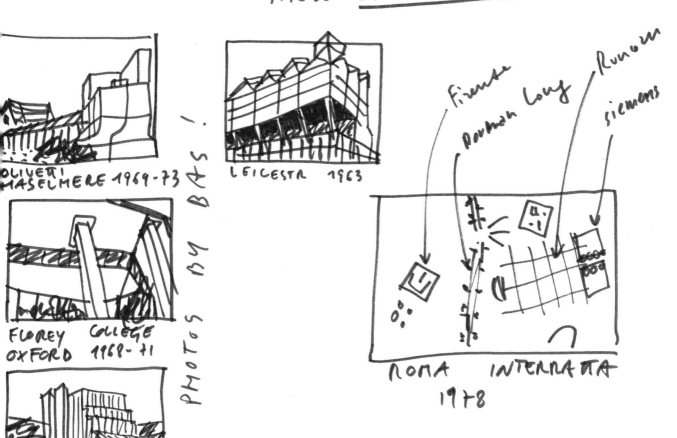

OLIVETTI HASELMERE 1969-73

LEICESTR 1963

FLOREY COLLEGE OXFORD 1958-71

PHOTOS BY BAS!

Firenze
Poulton Long
Runcorn
siemens

ROMA INTERRATA 1978

FACULTY OF HISTORY - CAMBRIDGE 1968

64

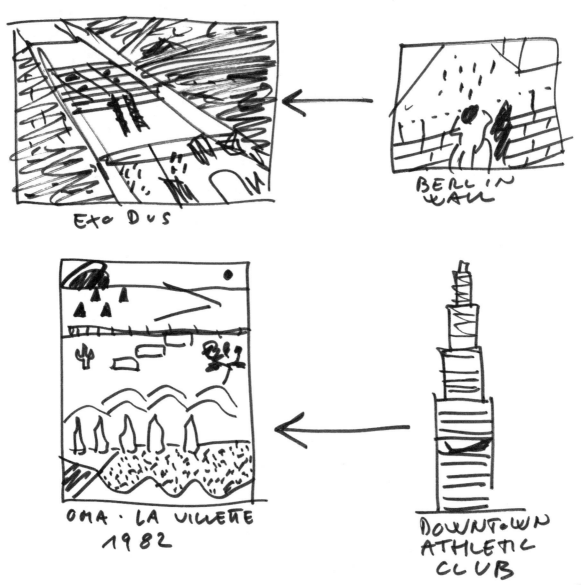

EXODUS

BERLIN WALL

OMA · LA VILLETTE
1982

DOWNTOWN
ATHLETIC
CLUB

The grand
proletarian
cultural
locomotive

?

1969
LEARNING FROM
LAS VEGAS
PRESENTATION
AA LONDON

DENISE

BOB

IN "LEARNING FROM L.V."
THE ARGUMENT BECOMES
PSEUDO - SOCIOLOGICAL AND
VAGUELY MORALISTIC.
THE BOOK IS CERTAINLY
BETTER WRITTEN THAN
"COMPLEXITY AND CONTRADIC-
TION", BUT THE ARCHITECTURE
BECOMES AN AFTERTHOUGHT
AND BECOMES PRISONER
OF COMMUNICATION (AND
So PRISONER OF CONTENT,
A BIZARRE DESTINY FOR
A FORMALIST LIKE VENTURI)

1976 VSBA

A BUILDING 16 FT HIGH AND
1100 FT LONG WITH ONLY
TWO DOORS AND NO WINDOWS

THIS SON OF A BITCH
IS CURZIO MALAPARTE

CHURCH IN LIPARI

LE MÉPRIS

↑
BRIGITTE

ROSSI

GHIRRI

THE DISCOVERY OF BEAUTY INTO THE
FAMILIAR LANDSCAPE

ROSSI SAN
NAZARO DE BURGUNDI

GHIRRI

L.C. LA TOURETTE

TROIS RAPPELS
A MESSIEURS LES ARCHITECTES
I
LE VOLUME

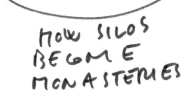

HOW SILOS
BECOME
MONASTERIES

A CLEF C'EST REGARDER:
REGARDER
OBSERVER
VOIR
IMAGINER
INVENTER
CRÉER

15.08.1963
(L.C. DIED 27.08.1965)

IN AN ENTIRELY
DIFFERENT
CULTURAL CONTEXT
(L.C. 1920S VS L.C.
1950S) THE SAME
FORMAL ELEMENTS
REAPPEARS.
FORMAL EDUCATION
VS IDEOLOGY

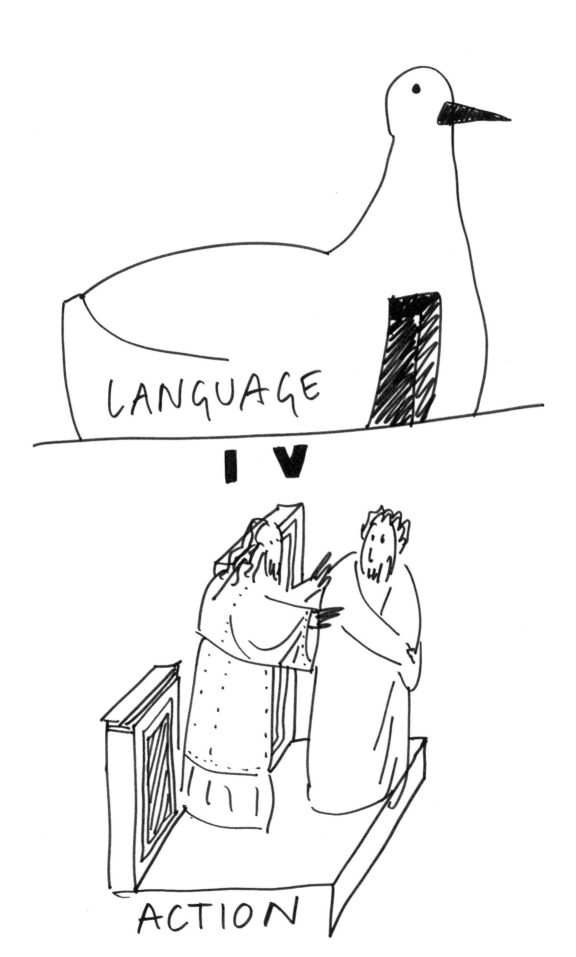

ARCHITECTURE AS
LANGUAGE, AS
SYMBOLISM

ARCHITECTURE
AS THE SETTING
FOR THE EXECUTION
OF AN ACTION

↑

DUCK
/
DECORATED
SHED

↓

"Any semiotic system works
out a code to transmit a message
and architecture does not
convey this message; the
information that can be
derived or somehow obtained
from it is not the message
that would assure its
semiotic nature"
C. Brandi, Struttura e
architettura, Torino: Einaudi
1967

VSB Football hall
of fame 1967

GIOTTO   1290 - 95 ca.

THE BACK OF
BILLBOARD   THE BACK OF
THE CROSS

THE "PROBLEM OF THE BACK" AS A
PROBLEM OF MAKING, AS THE
PROBLEM OF HUMAN WORK

ENZO MARI
HAMMER AND
SICKLE 1972

MARI 44 VALUTAZIONI
1977

MARI, IL RITRATTO
DI DIO

MARI, THE PORTRAIT OF
GOD. ALLEGORY. MIRROR,
TREE, ROCK, CALF, MEN

ABSENCE AS
AN ACTION
THE OBJECT IS
SIMPLY A TOOL TO
LET SOMETHING
ELSE APPEAR

ALDO ROSSI
SCUOLA DE
AMICIS BRONI
1969-71

SYMBOLISM BY
MEANS OF ABSENCE

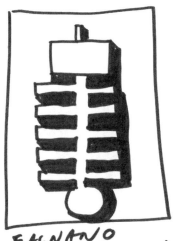

FAGNANO
OLONA SCUOLA
1972-76

THE CAPACITY
OF THE BUILDING
TO HOST A PRECISE
GESTURE

BUILDING IS BOTH
SYMBOL AND STAGE

BRONI   NEW
SCHOOL 1979

← THIS BUILDING IS <u>JUST</u>
A SYMBOL
ABIGUITY IS LOST
THE GESTURES THAT
SHOULD APPEAR ARE ALL
CAREFULLY NAMED

ROSSI BEFORE
MODENA CEMETERY
(1971)
    COLLECTIVE
    SPECTRES

/

ROSSI AFTER
MODENA CEMETERY
PRIVATE
SPECTRES

→ END OF HISTORY?

1989 FUKUOKA

THE EXPULSION OF ST. JOACHIM FROM THE TEMPLE SCROVEGNI CHAPEL 1303-05

THE TEMPLE IS MADE OF BALDACHIN + PULPIT+ PRAECINT WALL

The wall is the precondi for the expulsion There is no action here without architecture

THE TEMPLE IS ALWAYS MADE OF THE SAME PIECES: STAIRS, BALDACHIN, PULPIT, WALL. THESE ARE THE ELEMENTS THAT ALLOW ALL THE ACTIONS HAPPENING AT THE TEMPLE TO BE PERFORMED

THE PRESENTATION OF THE VIRGIN TO THE TEMPLE 1303-05

The relation among spatial boundaries and bodies inside is extremely tight. The walls are pressed onto bodies to force dramatic action "MIMIC BOXES"

While the buildings acquire a more realistic relation to people, the relation among space and action is lost

THE BUILDING IS NO MORE JUST A SET OF CONDITIONS FOR ACTION

TADDEO GADDI PRESENTATION OF THE VERGIN TO THE TEMPLE 1330S CAPPELLA BARONCELLI SANTA CROCE

"LANGUAGE"

THE LANGUAGE PIST MODERN ARCH

CHARLES JECKNCKS 1978 Piazza d'Italia New Orleans Charles Moore

ARCHITECTURE AS SIGN

.SUMMERSON, THE CLASSICAL LANGUAGE OF ARCHITECTURE, 1963

B.ZEVI THE MODERN LANGUAGE OF ARCHITECTURE, 1973

U. ECO, LA STRUTTURA ASSENTE 1968

ADOLPHE APPIA SCENE FOR TRISTAN UND ISOLDE 1923

ARCHITECTURE AS THE PRODUCTION OF A SCENE TO EXECUTE GESTURES, AS THE POSSIBILITY OF A GESTURE

2.0141 DIE MÖGLICHKEIT SEINES VORKOMMENS IN SACHVERHALTEN IST DIE FORM DES GEGENSTANDES

→ L. Wittgenstein, Tractatus logic-philosophicus, 1921

76

ROBERT BRESSON
PICKPOCKET 1959

THE MECHANIC STUPIDITY
OF WAR. THE FIRST MINUTES
OF THE MOVIE WITH ONLY
SOUND OF SWORDS BEATING
METAL ARMOUR.
THE SEQUENCE OF GESTURES
WITHOUT INTERPRETATION

LANCELOT DU LAC
1974

J. BALDESSARI
THROWING THREE
BALLS IN THE AIR
TO GET A STRAIGHT
LINE 1973

ROY LICHTENSTEIN
1962

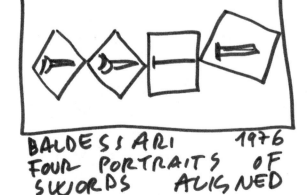

BALDESSARI 1976
FOUR PORTRAITS OF
SWORDS ALIGNED

MEANING IN ARCHITECTURE

L. JENCKS
G. BAIRD 1970

ACTION TAKING PLACE IN THE CITY →

GIULIO PAOLINI 1965
DIAFRAMMA 8

Paolini's problem : is still Giotto's problem : how to represent human acting in space

ACTION TAKING PLACE IN THE CITY AND REPRESENTATION OF ACTION TAKING PLACE IN THE CITY

PAOLINI D867 1967

HOW TO FRAME ACTION?
Paolini's problem : How to represent (public space)

CORNELIS GYSBRECHTS
CA. 1670

PAOLINI 1/25
1965

Paolini's problem is not only REPRODUCIBILITY not only STATUS OF THE ARTWORK as in so much modern and post-modern art, it is also REPRESENTATION OF SPACE and REPRESENTATION IN SPACE

VICTOR STOICHITA, THE SELF-AWARE IMAGE, 1997 (L'INSTAURATION DU TABLEAU, 1993)

The ~~erasure~~ of the historical architecture of the pre-existing station perceived as "Fascist". Note that Minoletti was a relatively commercial architect. The project can be understood only starting from the collective ethics of post-war Italy

GIULIO   MINOLETTI
EUGENIO GENTILI TEDESCHI
         1953
MILAN CENTRAL STATION

THE BUILDING AS A
GESTURE THAT CREATES
THE POSSIBILITY OF
OTHER GESTURES

J. BALDESSARI
TWO STARES MAKING
A POINT BUT BLOCKED
BY PLANE (FOR MALEVICH)
1976

QUARONI - RIDOLFI
STAZIONE TERMINI

(IT IS SO UGLY THAT IT
IS NOT EVEN POSSIBLE
TO RE-DRAW IT)

COMPETITION 1947

MONTUORI

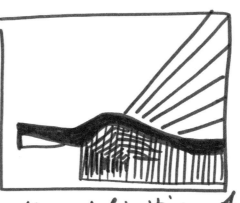

The attempt to _express_
the conditions/aspirations
of post-war Italy
the contradictory desire
for future and past, #2
monumentality and
anti-monumentality

the definition of
the _scale_ of a
new infrastructure

LANGUAGE NOT NECESSARILY
AS PRECISE COMMUNICATION
BUT AS AN INTENTION TO SPEAK

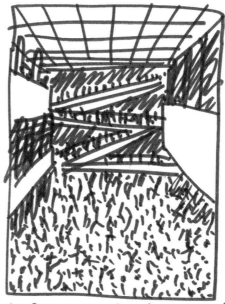

I. B. VILANOVA ARTIGAS
FAU SÃO PAULO 1961-68

80

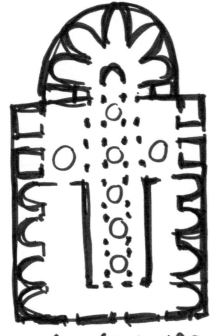

FRA GIOCONDO
PROJECT FOR ST. PETER'S

THE CHURCH PRECISELY
FOLLOWS THE RITUALS
PROVIDING SPECIFIC
SPACES FOR ALL
DIFFERENT FUNCTIONS
SPACE IS FRAGMENTED

POINT TO POINT
CORRESPONDENCE

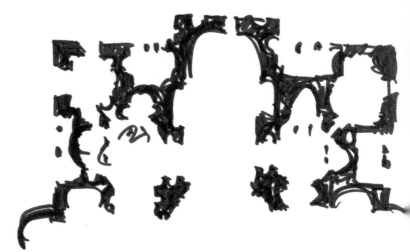

BRAMANTE UA 1

THERE IS NO CORRESPONDENCE
OF RITUALS TO SPACES; SPACE
CORRESPONDS TO THE RITUALS
AS A WHOLE (AND AS
A REPRESENTATION OF
SPACE, AS A "SPECTACLE
OF SPACE")

UNDIRECT CORRESPONDENCE

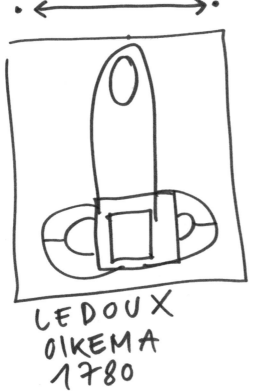

LEDOUX
OIKEMA
1780

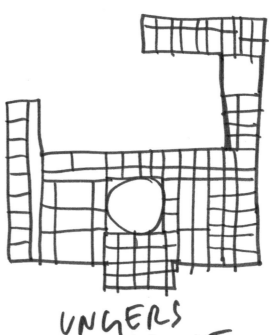

UNGERS
KARLSRUHE
LIBRARY
1980 - 84

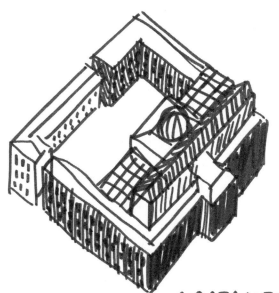

THE COMPLETE ABSTRACTION
OF THE PLAN TURNS INTO
EXTREME ~~REACH~~ IDENTITY
IN THE VOLUMETRIC
COMPOSITION.
TYPE BECOMES <u>MEANING</u>
(OR AT LEAST IT SEEMS O.M.U.
WOULD HAVE LIKED)

OIKEMA

THE PHALLIC ANALOGY
OF THE PLAN IS
COMPLETELY LOST
IN THE APPEARANCE
OF THE BUILDING

ARCHITECTURE
PARLANTE

BUILDINGS THAT "HAVE TO
ANNOUNCE THEIR PURPOSE
TO THE VIEWER"

Boffrand
Livre d'
architecture
1745

BOULLÉE 1784

THE SPHERE
BECOMES A
SYMBOL

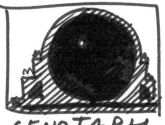

CENOTAPH
FOR NEWTON

THE INNER
ROOM PRODUCES
A CONDITION

"...Boullée putting <u>character</u> in a work signifies
using all the means at his disposal to
make sure we do not <u>perceive sensations</u>
<u>other than the ones intrinsic to the</u>
object." A. Rossi, Introduzione a Boullée, 1967

E. L. BOULLÉE ca. 1785
BIBLIOTHÈQUE DU ROI

BORIS IOFAN
PALACE OF SOVIETS 1932
CLASSICISM AS
A SYMBOL IN ITSELF

V. PAPERNY, CULTURE
TWO. ARCHITECTURE
IN THE AGE OF STALIN
2011

RAFFAELLO
SCUOLA DI ATENE

CLASSICISM AS THE
RELATION OF SPACE
TO GESTURES
THE VOLUMES OF AIR
IN THE BARREL VAULTS
ABOVE THE PHILOSOPHERS
IN THE SCHOOL OF ATHENS

THE MOST EXTREME
CONSEQUENCE OF
ROMAN ARCHITECTURE;
ONLY INTERIOR SPACE
MATTERS!
BRAMANTE'S
STR PETER'S

HAGIA SOPHIA
537 CE 558-62 RESTORED
869 BY BAU

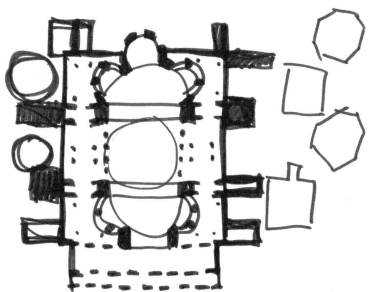

THE WILD ACCUMULATION
OF BUTTRESSES AROUND.
EXTERIOR SPACE IS
ENTIRELY SUBORDINATED TO
INTERIOR

PIERO DELLA FRANCESCA. DISCOVERY
AND PROOF OF THE TRUE CROSS
1460S
ALL FIGURES ARE WAITING FOR
ACTION TO TAKE PLACE. IMMOBILITY
IN PIERO'S PAINTING
(PAINTING DEALS WITH IMMOVABLE
THINGS)

DAVID HOCKNEY 1968
AMERICAN COLLECTORS

84

The comp... among 2 groups of buildings and 2 groups of people

GIOTTO CAPPELLA PERUZZI 1320 ca. RAISING OF DRUSIANA

THE RELATION OF SCENE AND GESTURE IS NOT LINEAR, AND IT IS RENEWED FOR ANY NEW GESTURE

(see evolution from "the Renunciation to the ~~earthly~~ Worldly Goods" in St. Francis' cycle in Assisi)

THE RELATION AMONG THE FO... IN THE CITY WALLS AND TH... TWO HANDS OF ST. JOHN AND DRUSIANA

G.E. ASPLUND 1928 LIBRARY

S. LEWERENTZ 1925 RESURRECTION CHAPEL

The same delicacy can appear as the suggestion of a message (Asplund, Sita) and as the preparation of a gesture (Lewerentz). The minor shift in plan of the Resurrection chapel and the minor alterations of Bensjou Interior.

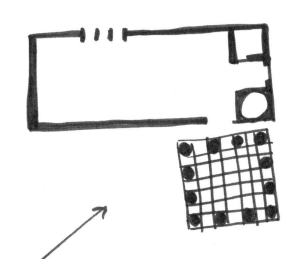

EARLY LEWERENTZ IS SO MUCH BETTER THAN LATE L.

THE PORCH AND
THE MAIN BODY
OF THE CHAPEL
ARE NOT PERFECTLY
ALIGNED. THERE
IS A GAP, ALMOST
IMPERCEPTIBLE

THE ACTION OF ENTERING IS
DETACHED FROM THE
ACTION OF BEING IN THE
CHURCH. THIS DIFFERENCE
IS NOT <u>DECLARED</u>, NOT
EVEN ANNOUNCED, IT SIMPLY
HAPPENS.

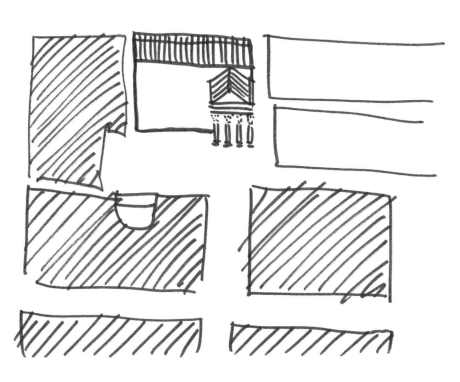

OLIMPIA

LANDSCAPE
AS A SET
OF POINTS
IN A
TERRITORY

MOUNT ATHOS AS IN THE
PROJECT BY DINOCRATES
(FISCHER VON ERLACH, ENTWURFF)
VITRUVIUS BOOK II, 1-4

LANDSCAPE AS ICON
(AND THE IMPOSSIBILITY FOR
LANDSCAPE TO BECOME ICON,
SEE MT. RUSHMORE TOO)

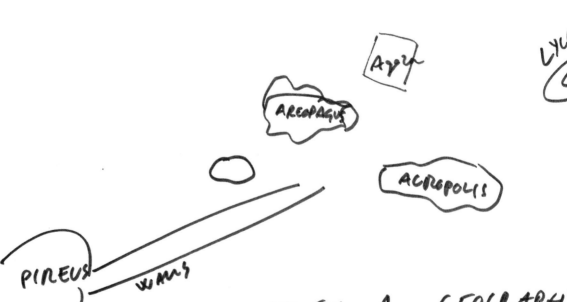

ATHENS, A GEOGRAPHY
OF POINTS WITH NO REAL
URBAN TISSUE IN BETWEEN

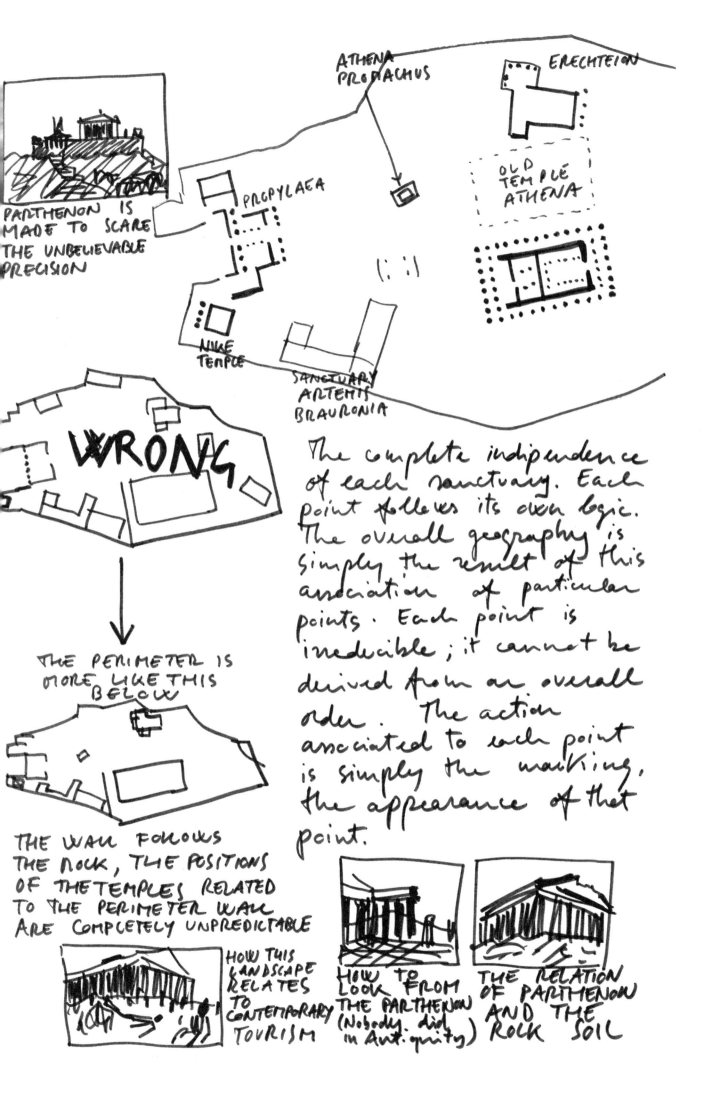

ATHENA PROMACHUS

ERECHTEION

OLD TEMPLE ATHENA

PARTHENON IS MADE TO SCARE THE UNBELIEVABLE PRECISION

PROPYLAEA

NIKE TEMPLE

SANCTUARY ARTEMIS BRAURONIA

WRONG

The complete independence of each sanctuary. Each point follows its own logic. The overall geography is simply the result of this association of particular points. Each point is irreducible; it cannot be derived from an overall order. The action associated to each point is simply the marking, the appearance of that point.

THE PERIMETER IS MORE LIKE THIS BELOW

THE WALL FOLLOWS THE ROCK, THE POSITIONS OF THE TEMPLES RELATED TO THE PERIMETER WALL ARE COMPLETELY UNPREDICTABLE

HOW THIS LANDSCAPE RELATES TO CONTEMPORARY TOURISM

HOW TO LOOK FROM THE PARTHENON (Nobody did in Antiquity)

THE RELATION OF PARTHENON AND THE ROCK SOIL

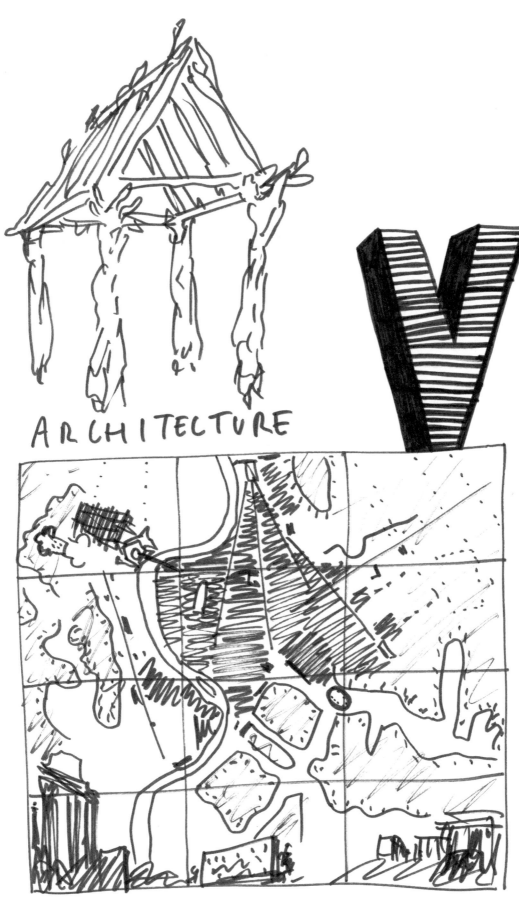

ARCHITECTURE

CITY

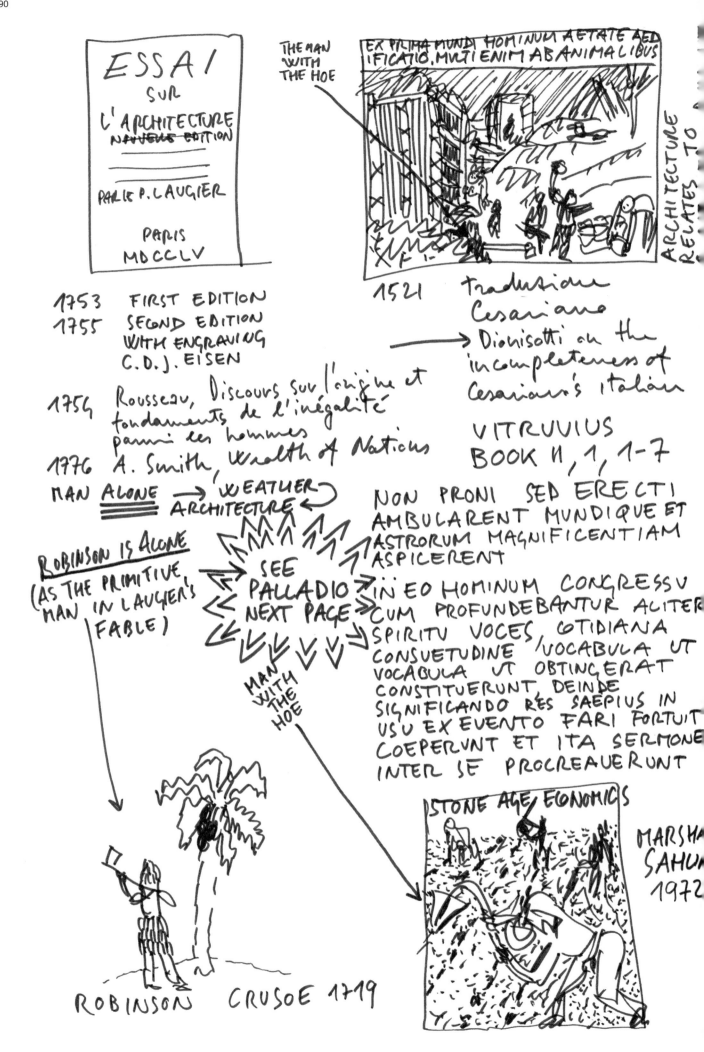

90

ESSAI
SUR
L'ARCHITECTURE
~~NOUVELLE EDITION~~
_____

PAR LE P. LAUGIER

PARIS
MDCCLV

THE MAN
WITH
THE HOE

EX PRIMA MUNDI HOMINUM AETATE AED
IFICATIO. MULTI ENIM AB ANIMALIBUS

ARCHITECTURE RELATES TO

1521 Traduzione Cesariano
→ Dionisotti on the incompleteness of Cesariano's italian

1753 FIRST EDITION
1755 SECOND EDITION WITH ENGRAVING C.D.J. EISEN

1754 Rousseau, Discours sur l'origine et fondaments de l'inégalité parmi les hommes

1776 A. Smith, Wealth of Nations

MAN ALONE → WEATHER ARCHITECTURE ←

VITRUVIUS
BOOK II, 1, 1-7

NON PRONI SED ERECTI
AMBULARENT MUNDIQUE ET
ASTRORUM MAGNIFICENTIAM
ASPICERENT

ROBINSON IS ALONE
(AS THE PRIMITIVE MAN IN LAUGIER'S FABLE)

SEE PALLADIO NEXT PAGE

IN EO HOMINUM CONGRESSU
CUM PROFUNDEBANTUR ALITER
SPIRITU VOCES, COTIDIANA
CONSUETUDINE VOCABULA UT
VOCABULA UT OBTINGERAT
CONSTITUERUNT, DEINDE
SIGNIFICANDO RES SAEPIUS IN
USU EX EVENTO FARI FORTUIT
COEPERUNT ET ITA SERMONE
INTER SE PROCREAUERUNT

MAN WITH THE HOE

STONE AGE ECONOMICS

MARSHA SAHU 1972

ROBINSON CRUSOE 1719

"ONE MAN [...] HAS MORE OF A CERTAIN COMMODITY THAN HE HIMSELF HAS OCCASION FOR, FOR, WHILE ANOTHER HAS LESS. THE FORMER CONSEQUENTLY WOULD BE GLAD TO DISPOSE OF, AND THE LATER TO PURCHASE, A PART OF THIS SUPERFLUITY"

WEALTH OF NATIONS, BOOK I, 4

1922
MARCEL MAUSS,
ESSAI SUR LE DON, 1925

KARL POLANYI,
THE GREAT TRANSFORMA-
TION, 1944

KARL POLANYI, PRIMITIVE
ARCHAIC AND MODERN
ECONOMICS, 1968

Exchange takes place in between societies, not individuals

VITRUVIUS, BOOK IV, 1

CALLIMACHUS CONE UENTS CORINTHIAN CAPITAL

ROLAND FREART DE CHAMBRAY 1650
PARALLÈLE DE L'ARCHITECTURE ANTIQUE AVEC LA MODERNE

The possibility to define a single origin for architectural needs or decisions

"ATOMISTIC" APPROACH
Nadio . Alberti . Laugier . Semper

PLANET OF THE APES
Pierre Boulle 1963
F. J. Schaffner 1968

the relation among an entire civilisation and architecture
"ARCHITECTURE, PROPERLY UNDERSTOOD, IS CIVILIZATION ITSELF" (W.R. Lethaby

"DIALECTIC APPROACH"
Fischer . Rossi . Koolhaas . Loos

ALBINI - HELG
NOORDA 1963
(VIGNELLI)

⎰ M1 MILANO
⎱ This was Rossi's
  Milan /a <u>modern</u> city

1966
L'ARCHITETTURA
DELLA CITTÀ
MOVE PAST "NAIVE FUNCTIONAL

| ALL FUNCTIONALISM IS NANE FUNCTIONALISM |

CASTIGLIONI · THE
PESTICIDES PAVILION · 1955

CITY MADE OF ARCHITECTURE

↓

ALDO ROSSI STARES
AT STALIN - MOSKOW
1954

ROLE
OF
STALINIS
ARCHITE
IN RUSS
CRITIUSM

SÍ PERCHÉ SI DEVE CREDERE CHE
QUELLE (LE CASE DEI PARTICOLARI) AI
PUBBLICI EDIFICII LE RAGIONI SOMMI-
NISTRASSERO, ESSENDO MOLTO VERISIMILE,
CHE INNANZI, L'HUOMO DA PER SE
HABITASSE, E DOPO VEDENDO AVER
MESTIERI DELL'AIUTO DE GLI ALTRI
HUOMINI, A CONSEGUIR QUELLE COSE
CHE LO POSSONO RENDER FELICE
(SE FELICITÀ ALCUNA SI TROVA QUA
GIÙ) LA COMPAGNIA DE GLI ALTRI
HUOMINI NATURALMENTE DESIDE-
RASSE, E AMASSE: ONDE DI MOLTE
CASE SI FECERO LI BORGHI, E DI
MOLTI BORGHI POI LE CITTÀ, E IN QUELLE
I LUOGHI E GLI EDIFICIJ PUBBLICHI
[...] IO DUNQUE TRATTERÒ PRIMA
DELLE CASE PRIVATE, E VERRÒ POI
A' PUBBLICI EDIFICIJ
   PALLADIO, PROEMIO, P. 6

ARCHITECTURE
PRESUPPOSES
THE CITY

The Architecture <u>OF</u>
the City

SUBJECTIVE/OBJECTIVE
GENITIVE

ARCHITECTURE OF THE
CITY AS

LOOS + LEVI STRAUS

ROSSI
BRIDGE XIII
TRIENNALE
1964

HART
STAM
CHAIR S33
1926

TREES IS A PHOTOCOPY
FROM SCHINKEL

ROSSI . IAN NAZAR

BEITRÄGE ZUM BAUEN

1926   STAM.
HANNES MEYER. HANS
SCHMIDT. EL LISSITZKY

"STÄDTE ZU"
VERMIETEN"

"WHEN CHANGING PLACE
OF RESIDENCE, IT IS NO LONGER
NECESSARY TO PACK THE
FURNITURE VAN, ONLY THE
LUGGAGE"
     HILBERSEIMER. 1927
  &GROSSSTADTARCHITEKTUR

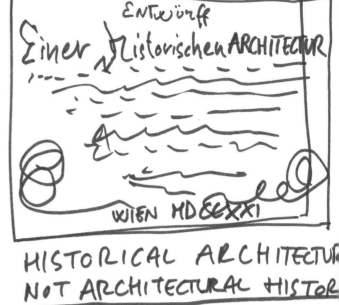

HISTORICAL ARCHITECTURE
NOT ARCHITECTURAL HISTOR

"OF ANTIQUITY AND OF FOREIGN
PEOPLE" (DES ALTERTUMS
UND FREMDER VÖLKER)

"BAU-ART DER ALTEN JÜDEN, AE
GYPTER, SYRER, PERSER UND
GRIECHEN"
     86   FOLIOS — 5 BOOKS

— HOW TO TRANSLATE
"ENTWURFF"

"UNE IDÉE GENERALE DE
LA DIVERSITÉ DES BATIMENT
DE L'ANTIQUITÉ ET DE TOUTES
LES NATIONS"

HANNES   MEYER
COOP - ROOM   1926

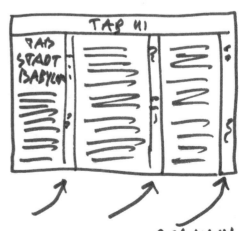

COLUMN FOR
SOURCES
FISCHER IS VERY ACCURATE

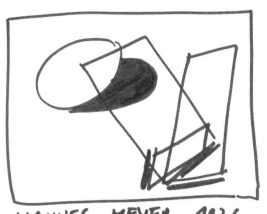

EGGS

HANNES MEYER 1926

FELICE CASORATI
UOVA SUL CASSETTONE
1920

SOCIETE' DES NATIONS
1927 HANNES MEYER
HANS WITTWER

EGG

PIERO DELLA
FRANCESCA
PALA MONTEFELTRO

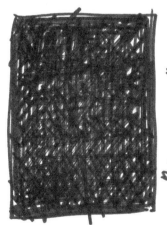

"CONTEXT"

CHRISTOPHER
ALEXANDER
NOTES ON THE
SYNTHESIS
OF FORM
1964

HANGING GARDENS
OF BABYLON

7 WONDERS

SEVEN WONDERS ARE
SEVEN

A PLURAL COLLECTION

ALAIN RESNAIS
L'ANNÉE DERNIÈRE A
MARIENBAD   1961

SEA RANCH   1970
CHARLES MOORE
DONLYN LYNDON
LAWRENCE HALPRIN

ANNA HALPRIN
DANCE SEMINARS
"MOVEMENT RITUALS"

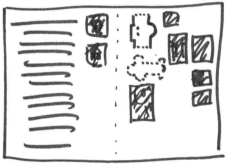

ROBERT VENTURI
"COMPLEXITY AND
CONTRADICTION IN
ARCHITECTURE"
1966

COMPLEXITY SHOULD
BE ADDED BY MEANS
OF ARCHITECTURE

CANALETTO

FOR ROSSI COMPLEXITY IS
ALREADY IN THE CITY
AND ARCHITECTURE PRESUPPOSE
SUCH COMPLEXITY

SO IT HAS TO BE SIMPLE!

THE MODERNIST
GRAPHIC DESIGN OF
VENTURI

FISCHER PYRAMIDS

RICHTER
THEY BOTH
REPRESENT THE
MEMORY OF THE
OBJECT MORE THAN
THE OBJECT ITSELF

G
MATERIAL
ZUR ELEMENTAREN
GESTALTUNG
N.3 1924

THE ABSOLUTE
AUTONOMY OF THE OBJECT

FISCHER
MAUSOLEUM OF
ALICARNASSUS

THE OBJECT INCORPORATES THE
COMPLEXITY OF ITS CONTEXT

98

HANS KOLLHOFF 1982
MUSEUM OF ANTHROPOLOGY
FRANKFURT A.M.
The possibility for
the object to become
city

KOLLHOFF · POTSDAMERPLATZ
PROPOSAL · 1992
CAPITALIST REALISM

KOLLHOFF · WALTER BENJAMIN
PLATZ · BERLIN · 2000

FISCHER V.E. - COLOSSUS OF
RHODES
P.A. Clayton, M. Price, The
Seven Wonders of the Ancient
World, 1989

FISCHER - NILE WATERFALLS

RICHTER   NIAGARA
1965

INIGO JONES   1655
THE MOST NOTABLE ANTIQUITY OF GREAT BRITAIN

Fischer
Stonehenge
+
Natural
Rock
near
Salisbury

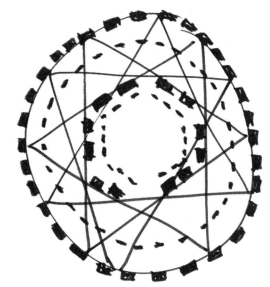

FOR INIGO JONES
STONEHENGE IS A ROMAN
RUIN

MADELON VRIESENDORP
OMA. THE TALE OF
THE POOL 1977

THE
EXTREMELY
ELONGATED
PERSPECTIVE

FISCHER · ISOLA BELLA

ONLY
REAL
BUILDINGS

SULTAN AHMED

ONLY
MONUMENTAL
BUILDINGS

MECCA

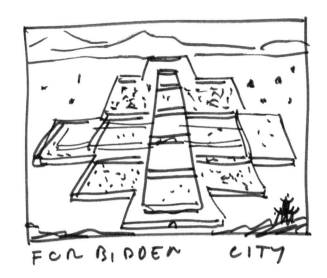

FORBIDDEN CITY

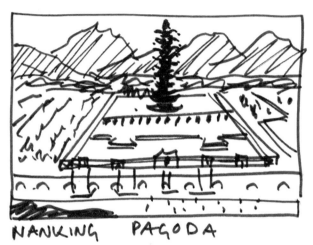

NANKING PAGODA

"ONE MIGHT BEGIN A
BOOK ON ANTHROPOLOGY IN
THIS WAY: WHEN WE WATCH
THE LIFE AND BEHAVIOUR
OF MEN ALL OVER THE
EARTH, WE SEE THAT
APART FROM WHAT WE
MIGHT CALL ANIMAL
ACTIVITIES, TAKING FOOD,
ETC., ETC. MEN ALSO CARRY
OUT ACTIONS THAT BEAR
A PECULIAR CHARACTER
AND MIGHT BE CALLED
RITUALISTIC "

WITTGENSTEIN, NOTES
ON FRAZER'S GOLDEN
BOUGH

102

HILBERSEIMER . 1928
DEVELOPMENT FRIEDRICHSTADT
THE NEW BEGINNING. THE
AESTHETIC QUALITY OF THE
PROJECT IS IN THE
UNDERSTANDING OF THE
RHYTM OF FRIEDRICHSTADT
BUT ALSO IN THE ERASURE
OF IT.

ROME AGE OF COSTANTINE
306 - 337 . MODEL
ITALO GISMONDI - 1935-71

HANNES MEYER. HANS WITTWER
PETERSCHULE. BASEL 1926
(PERSPECTIVE DRAWING SOMETIMES
ATTRIBUTED TO PAUL KLEE)

The clearest alternative
among an architecture
derive from the city
and a (new, modern)
architecture based on

MIES VAN DER ROHE
REICHSBANK . 1933
The capacity to read
the measure (the rhytm)
of the city and turn
it into building / the
relation of the building
to the river running
behind it

program and constitution
for the city is, in the
story of Bernini's travel
to France to build the
Louvre   1665

LOUIS XIV

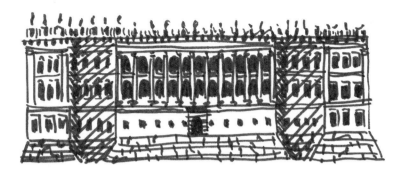

GIAN LORENZO BERNINI
LOUVRE III PROJECT

65. LOUIS XIV IS 26
COLBERT IS 45
BERNINI IS 66

P. FRÉART DE CHANTELOU,
JOURNAL DU VOYAGE DU
CAV. BERNINI EN FRANCE

COLBERT

BERNINI
(OLD)

5 SEPTEMBER 1665
BERNINI TALKS
TO THE ACADEMY
AND SAYS THAT
STUDENTS MUST STUDY
ANCIENT MASTERPIECES
FIRST AND, ONLY
AFTER THAT, NATURE

IN 1665 BERNINI
IS NO MORE THE
SENSUAL ARTIST
OF THIS "RAPE
OF PROSERPINA"
(1622)

BERNINI'S CARICATURE OF
DYING ~~DIES~~ POPE ALEXANDER VII

PHOTO
ALINARI
1922

"OH QUANTO MI VERGOGNO
DI AVER OPERATO COSÍ
MALE"
OLD BERNINI ON HIS
FOUNTAIN OF THE
FOUR RIVERS 1648-51
D. BERNINI, VITA DEL
CAVALIER GIO. LORENZO
BERNINO, 1713

ST. PETER'S SQUARE
BERNINI STARTS
WORKING IN 1656
ALEXANDER VII (POPE 1655-
1667)

WHEN IN PARIS, BERNINI
IS STILL CONCERNED BY
THE CONSTRUCTION OF
ST. PETER'S SQUARE

BERNINI
PORTRAIT
OF LOUIS XIV

(THE KING IS
THE ONLY MEMBER
OF THE COURT
WHO ESTABLISHED
AN ACCEPTABLE
RELATION WITH
BERNINI)

LOUVRE - HALF SECTION
II PROJECT

LOUVRE - COLONNADE   CLAUDE PERRAULT   1668 - 80 CA.
(LOUIS XIV LEAVES LOUVRE CA. 1682)

THE RHYTH OF THE CITY / THE FLOW OF THE WATER. SEE MIES VAN DER ROHE REICHSBANK

3   10   3w   10   1   7

THE ASYMMETRY OF BERNINI'S RIVER FAÇADE IS NOT UNDERSTANDABLE FOR PERRAULT. ON 6 OCTOBER PERRAULT CRITICIZES THE FAÇADE; BERNINI FEELS INSULTED AND ASKS THE KING TO LEAVE.

OBJECTIONS BY COLBERT / PERRAULT: HOW TO INTRODUCE MACHINES FOR SPECTACLES IN THE COURTYARD (15 JULY); PARKING FOR MILITARY CARRIAGES (30 JULY); FIRE PROTECTION (11 AUGUST; 15 OCTOBER); CORRESPONDENCE AMONG "ETIQUETTE OF THE COURT" AND BUILDING ORGANIZATION (30 JULY, 21 AUGUST, 6 OCTOBER) [TO THIS BERNINI ASWERS THAT HE BETTER ASK THE "MARECHAL DE LOGIS" AND THAT AT THE VATICAN PALACE THE ARRANGEMENT OF THE ROOMS CHANGES WITH EVERY POPE].

COCK

CHARLES LE BRUN
ORDRE FRANÇAIS
GALERIE DES GLACES, VERSAILLES
1678

1671 COMPETITION FOR A NEW "FRENCH ORDER" 3000 LIVRES

CORN ORDER
U.S. CAPITOL
B.H. LATROBE

SAME STAIRS
AS MEYER'S PETER SCHULE
(MAYBE THROUGH ALBINI'S
FIRST PROPOSAL FOR
RINASCENTE IN ROME)

"MITTERAND'S
"GRAND
PROJETS"
LAST LAR
SCALE PUB
COMMISSIO
IN EUROP

BEAUBOURG

PROJECT
1983

LOUVRE   PYRAMID
I. M. PEI   1988

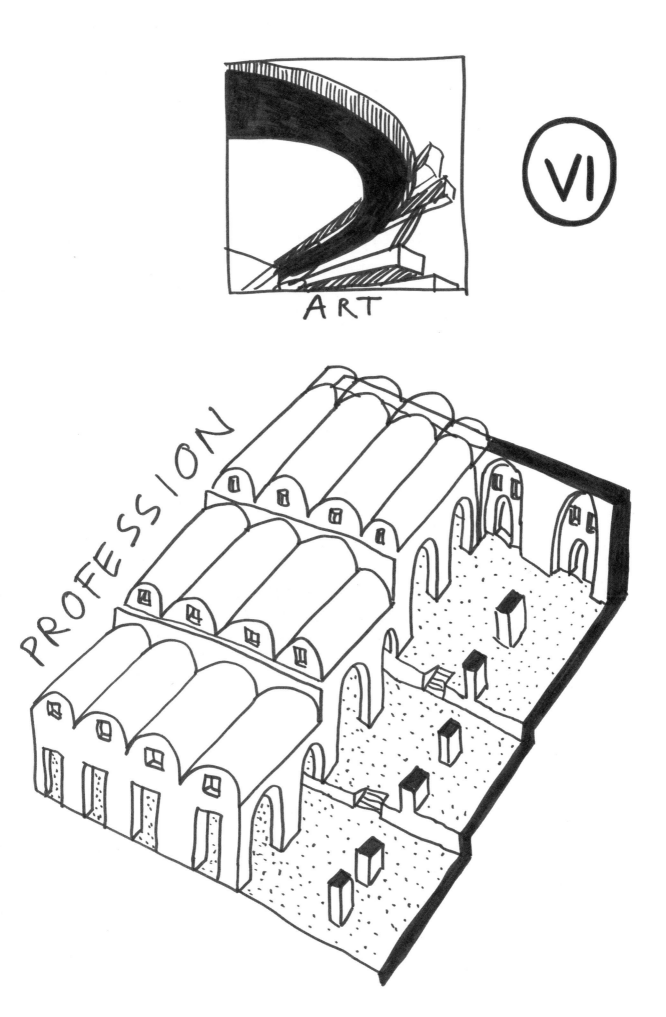

ART

VI

PROFESSION

SOM (?) OFFICE 1960S

HANS POELZIG BY AUGUST SANDER 1929

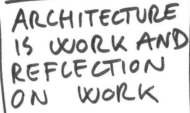

ARCHITECTURE IS WORK AND REFLECTION ON WORK

ARCHITECTURE IS THE ONLY WAY TO THINK ABOUT ARCHITECTURE

MCKIM · MEAD & WHITE 1879 · 1906

ARCHITECTURE AS MACROSCOPIC CONSEQUENCE OF A PROCESS OF INSTITUTIONALIZATION HADID

M. TAFURI, TOWARDS A CRITIQUE OF ARCHITECTURAL IDEOLOGY 196

ARCHITECTURE IS EXPLOITATION AND OPPRESSION (LINK TO "AGRICULTURAL REVOLUTION", WRITING ORGANIZED BUREAUCRACY)

ARCHITECTURE AS THE THE ONLY WAY TO EXPOSE ~~THESE~~ THE SPATIAL ASPECTS OF THIS VERY OPPRESSION.

SCENE FROM "THE TEN COMMANDMENTS" CECIL. B. ~~DE~~ DEMILLE 1956

ARCHITECTURE AS CONTROL OVER IMMENSE RESOURCES. PUBLIC BY DEFINITION

TAFURI: THERE CAN BE NO "ANTI-SPA ONLY CRITIQUE OF THE IDEOLOGY REALIZED IN ARCHITECT

WORKERS AT QATAR
WORLD CUP
CA. 6000 DEAD WORKERS
2010-2020
(MAINLY FROM INDIA,
PAKISTAN, BANGLADESH,
NEPAL, SRI LANKA')

YET ARCHITECTURE IS NOT
PURELY POWER, BUT
FORMALIZATION OF GIVEN
POWER.
PARS IMPERABANT, PARS
ARCHITECTABANTUR
(DANTE, DE VULGARI
ELOQUENTIA I, VII)

ARCHITECTURE IS POLITICAL
WORK, BUT IT DOES NOT
SOLVE POLITICAL PROBLEMS.
ARCHITECTURE IS POLITICAL
WORK ONLY INDIRECTLY,
AS ART, AS REPRESENTATION

REPRESENTATION / ~~VORGESTELLTEN~~ VERTRETEN
\ DAR-STELLEN

THE POSSIBILITY
TO REPRESENT
IS LINKED TO
THE SEPARATION,
THE GAP AMONG
REPRESENTED
AND REPRESENTATIVE

F. ANKERSMIT AESTHETIC
POLITICS: POLITICAL
PHILOSOPHY BEYOND FACT
AND VALUE, STANFORD,
1996

"WHAT COMES TO DEFINE
ARCHITECTURE IN HISTORY -
AT LEAST THAT OF WHAT WE
CALL WESTERN CIVILIZATION -
IS THE PROJECT THAT SOCIETY
IMPOSES ON ITSELF AND
WHICH THE BUILDER
REPRESENTS IN A BUILDING
ARTIGAS, ARQUITECTURA
E COMUNICAÇÃO, 1970

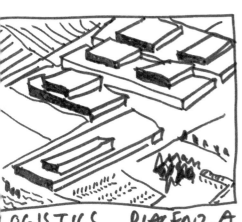

LOGISTICS PIACENZA
ARCHITECTURE IS
PUBLIC JUST BECAUSE OF
THE SCALE OF RESOURCES
T MOBILIZE.
(EXCEPTIONAL AMONG ARTS)

ARTIGAS FAU

AGUIRRE, DER ZORN
GOTTES 1972
(W. HERZOG)

RECONSTRUCTION
ST PETER'S

COLONIALISM

DIALOGUE
WITH ANCIENTS

DENIAL OF COEVALISM

(SEE ALSO LETTER MACHIAVELLI)
TO VETTORI

BRAMANTE
1444 - 1514
COLUMBUS
1451 - 1506
VESPUCCI
1454 - 1512

BRAMANTE 1506

WRONG
(SORRY)
SORT OF (

BRAMANTE   VA1
1506

J. FABIAN, TIME AND THE
OTHER: HOW
ANTHROPOLOGY MA
ITS OBJECT, NEW
1983

BRAMANTE   JULIUS II
(HARRY ANDREWS   (REX HARRISON)

C. REED, THE AGONY AND THE
ECSTASY, 1965
MICHELANGELO (CHARLTON HESTON)

KING VIDOR, THE
FOUNTAIN HEAD, 1949
(FROM AYN RAND'S BOOK
*

*AYN RAND IS A REPUGNANT FASCIST

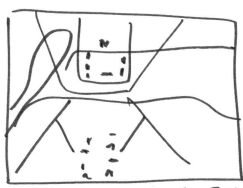

LE CORBUSIER SKETCH
ADDIS ABABA 1936
LETTER TO MUSSOLINI
19.08.1936
A PLAN FOR THE
CAPITAL OF THE
"AFRICA ORIENTALE
ITALIANA"

LE CORBUSIER
AMONG DOMINICAN MONKS
1956 - 60

BALDACHIN   BERNINI
ST PETER'S   +
1623-1634   BORROMINI

COLUMNS 20M HIGH

114

APPARATUS FOR CANONIZATION ST. FRANCIS OF SALES - 1665 - DE ROSSI

BALDACHIN ST. PETER 1624-33
"LE COSE NON APPAIONO SOLO
PER CIO' CHE SONO, MA IN
RELAZIONE ALLE COSE CHE
HANNO INTORNO, CHE NE
MODIFICANO L'APPARENZA "
                    BERNINI TO CHANTELO

MISURE DELLI ORI
MESSI DA DIVERSI SPADARI
A FOG SOPRA LI RAMI E
METALLI DEL ALTARE MAGGIORE
1632-33 (SEE M.G. D'AMELIO,
G.L. BERNINI E GLI ORI DEL BALDACCHINO DI S. PIETRO)

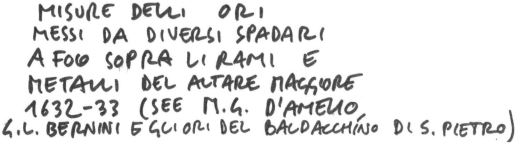

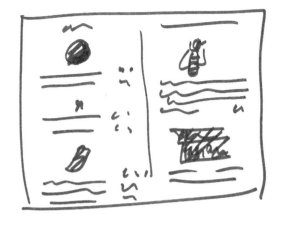

VINCENT DE RIJK

STATUE MODELS FOR OMA
CONSTANTINE

ERNINI TRIES NOT TO
XASPERATE THE PERSPECTIVE
FFECT

SCALA REGIA
THE CAPACITY TO ADAPT
TO ALL CIRCUSTANCES

BERNINI SCALA
REGIA

THE
HUMILITY
OF CAV.
BERNINI

BALTHASAR NEUMANN
AS COLONEL OF THE
MINI-ARMY OF THE
PRINCE-BISHOP OF   CANNON
WÜRZBURG
(DETAIL FROM TIEPOLO'S
APOLLO AND THE FOUR CONTINENTS)
NEUMANN'S
DOG

HANNES MEYER
(CONSIDER DRESS CODE)

PAUL ARTARIA / HANS
SCHMIDT HOUSE HUBER 1928

ALTHOUGH AT THE TIME
RADICAL, THIS TODAY
LOOKS LIKE A RATHER
COMMONSENSICAL, PRAGMATIC
HOUSE (WHAT IT WANTED
TO BE?). HERE THERE'S
NOTHING OF THE RADICALISM
OF STAM AND MEYER.

(AND THIS IS NOT PURELY RELATED
TO BIOGRAPHY: SCHMIDT WENT
TO USSR AS WELL AS MEYER)
THIS IS A PURELY
ARCHITECTURAL JUDGEMENT

ARTARIA / SCHMIDT
HOUSE SCHÄFFER 1927·28

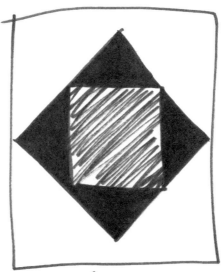

MAX BILL

MEYER
WITTWER

SOCIÉTÉ
DES
NATIONS
1927

BY RADICALLY RENOUNCING
ART, MEYER AND WITTWER
PARADOXICALLY MOVE ARCHITECTURE
IN THE (UNWELCOMING) REALM
OF CONCEPTUAL ART

118

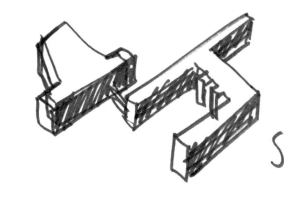

L.C

S.D.

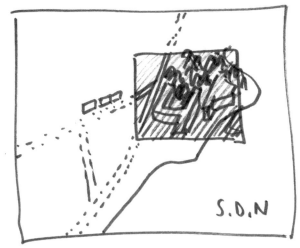

S.D.N

S.D.
POEL

ATELIER 5 . SIEDLUNG
HALEN — BERN 1961

MODERNISM BECOMING
A PLAIN STYLISTIC
SOLUTION THAT CAN
BE APPLIED IN EVERY
CIRCUMSTANCE (POST
"INTERNATIONAL STYLE")
SO MODERNISM LOSES ALL
AVANT-GARDE FLAVOUR
AND CAN BE USED AS
SIMPLE, PLAIN, COMMON
ARCHITECTURAL STYLE

LEVER HOUSE
1950 SOM

SEAGRAM BUILDING
1957
MIES VAN DER ROHE

HERE THE PROFESSIONAL
VERSION COMES BEFORE
AND THE AVANTGARDE ONE
AFTER. PROOF THAT WHAT SIMPLY
COMES FIRST DOES NOT MATTER THAT MUCH

THE
SPACE
THAT SEAGRAM
LEAVES

BURNHAM
McKIM

ARCHITECTS   CHICAGO
WORLD FAIR   1893

THE LAST METROPOLITAN
PROJECT FOR USA

ALTHOUGH APPARENTLY
SUCCESFUL BURNHAM AND
McKIM'S IDEA OF THE AMERICAN
CITY WOULD BE OBLITERATED
BY THE ROMANTIC/INDIVIDUALIST/
NATURE-INSPIRED IDEOLOGY OF
SULLIVAN AND F.L. WRIGHT
(VIA HENRY FORD AND AYN RAND)

LOUIS HENRY
SULLIVAN

SELF-PROCLAIMED
LOSERS WHO
ACTUALLY WIN

OLD F.L. WRIGHT

WHAT A
UGLY
DRAWING

CONCOURSE · PENN STATION
MC KIM - MEAD - WHITE 1910
COPY OF TEMPIDARIUM OF
CARACALLA BATHS (+20%)

D. BURNHAM · FLATIRON
NEW YORK. 1902

GRAND

THE DISTANCE OF COLUMNS
FROM WALLS BEHIND VARIES
ON ALL SIDES

MM&W
BOWERY
SAVINGS
BANK

THE
ABILITY
TO READ
THE
CADASTRAL
MAP

BOWERY

MMW DOES NOT LEAVE A SINGLE
CORNER UNUSED / THIS BECOMES
A SORT OF MEDITATION ON THE
REALITY OF THE CAPITALISTIC
CITY ~ AN ALMOST RELIGIOUS
RESPECT FOR THE SMALL
IRREGULARITIES OR GIVEN IN
THE CITY

MILOS FORMAN, RAGTIME, 1981
(PARTIALLY BASED ON THE
STORY OF THE ASSASSINATION
OF STANFORD WHITE)

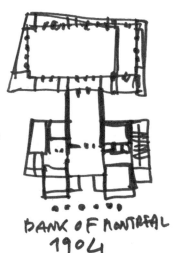

BANK OF MONTREAL
1904

WHITE
MURDERED
DURING
OPERETTA
AT MADISON
SQUARE
GARDEN 1906

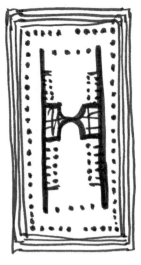

RUINS TEMPLE
VENUS AND ROME
BUILT UNDER HADRIAN
135 & CE (HADRIAN WAS APPARENTLY
ALSO THE ARCHITECT)
THE WORK WAS HEAVILY
CRITICIZED BY APOLLODORUS
OF DAMASCUS FOR NOT INCLUDING
STORAGE FOR THE MACHINERY
NECESSARY TO THE NEARBY COLISEUM.
THIS IS THE ONLY "DEBATE" AMONG
ROMAN ARCHITECTS OF WHICH
WE HAVE RECORD. ⟶
VERY INTERESTING THAT THE ONLY
"DEBATE" IN ROMAN ARCHITECTURE
THAT ARRIVED TO US IS ABOUT
STORAGE

HADRIAN SEN
APOLLODORUS I
EXILE AND THE
LET HIM BE
KILLED BECAU
OF HIS CRITICIS

SEE DIO CASSIUS, ROMAN HISTORY
VOL VIII: BOOK 69, 4 - 5.2

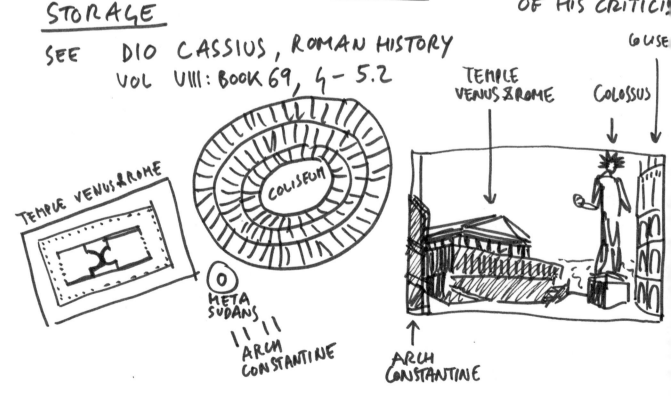

SOM - PEPSI COLA COMPANY
1958-60

VENTURI & RAUCH
TRANSPORTATION
SQUARE BUILDING
1968

MOLINE · ILLINOIS

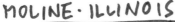

SAARINEN - ROCHE
JOHN DEERE HEADQUARTERS

GORDON BUNSHAFT
WAS PART OF THE
WASHINGTON FINE ARTS
COMMISSION AND OPPOSED
THE BUILDING
"UGLY AND ORDINARY"

(HERE IS THE HYPER-INTELLECTUAL
ARCHITECT - VENTURI - WHO
ADVOCATES COMPROMISE AND
CONTEXTUALISM AGAINST THE
MODERNIST PROFESSIONAL -
BUNSHAFT)

THE QUALITY OF AMERICAN CORPORATE
OFFICES OF THE 50S - 60S / RELATION
TO POLITICAL CONDITIONS ? LYNDON
JOHSON'S "BIG SOCIETY" - SEE ALSO THE
WORK OF DIRKERTS. THE POLITICAL
CONTEXT INFLUENCE ALSO
CORPORATIONS

THIS THING IS SHINY BLUE (ALL OF IT)

PACIFIC DESIGN CENTER
L.A.   CESAR PELLI
1975

ED RUSCHA
1962

RELATION AMONG CORPORATE COMMERCIAL PRODUCTION AND CONTEMPORARY ART

THIS IS A BLU

F. O. GEHRY — HOUSE L.A.
1978   SANTA MONICA

HERZOG DE MEURON
RICOLA STORAGE 1986-87

CARL ANDRE BUILDING
CEDAR PIECE 1964

HERZOG AND DE MEURON'S
INTEREST FOR MINIMALIST
ART WAS ALSO A WAY OUT
FROM THE DEAD END OF
LATE POST-MODERNISM
(HDM BOTH STUDIED WITH ROSSI
IN ZÜRICH)
THIS ANYHOW IMPLIED A
HEAVY DE-INTELLECTUALIZATION
OF THE PROFESSION
(MORE THAN WELCOMED IN A
NEO-LIBERAL CONTEXT)

MINIMALIST ART
WAS ALREADY
ENOUGH A-POLITICAL
ON ITS OWN

THE THEATRICALITY
OF MINIMAL ART

M. FRIED, ART AND
OBJECTHOOD, ART
FORUM, 1967

"AN EPISODE "IN THE HISTORY
OF SENSIBILITY"

AGAINST PAINTING, AGAINST
INVESTIGATION OF RELATIONS
INSIDE THE SPACE OF
THE PAINTING
"YOU SHOULD HAVE A DEFINITE
WHOLE AND MAYBE NO PARTS,
OR VERY FEW"   JUDD IN
                FRIED 1967

AGNES MARTIN ON ABSTRACT EXPRESSIONISTS:
"THEY WERE THE GREATEST ONES. THEY FREED PAINTING
FROM SPACE AND LET PAINTINGS BECOME THINGS. IN THE
BIG BLACK PAINTINGS OF (CLYFFORD) STILL, THE BLACK ISN'T
A PASSAGE OF SPACE, IT'S A THING. POLLOCK, ROTHKO,
DE KOONING, NEWMANN, ALL LIBERATED PAINTING
FROM THE SPACE OF A ROOM"

THE ANTI-INTELLECTUALISM
OF MINIMAL ART BECOMES
SO MUCH THE CURRENT
STANDARD THAT THE
ONLY ALTERNATIVE LEF
SEEMS TO BE ⌐

CARL ANDRE
ACQUITTED OF MURDERING
HIS WIFE ANA MENDIETA

O.J. SIMPSON
ACQUITTED OF MUR
HIS WIFE NICOLE B

MORALISM
OF WHICHEVER
SORT

HERZOG DE MEURON
HOUSING BASEL HEBELSTRASSE 1984-88

126

DELUXE APHASIA
OR
IDENTITY ACTIVISM
OR
BOTH
(ANYHOW NO "PUBLIC ART")

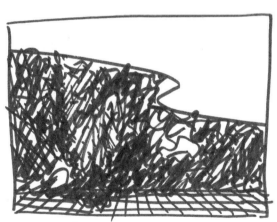

LUISA LAMBRI
NIEMEYER CASA DAS CANOAS

VII $\dfrac{\text{FIGURE}}{\text{GROUND}}$

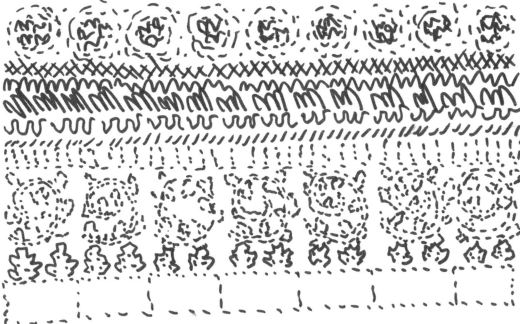

RICHARD MEIER
HOUSE DOUGLAS
1973

CORDOBA MOSQUE

A. GEHLEN, MAN: HIS NATU
AND PLACE IN THE WORLD,
ENG. TRANS, 1988

THE PREFERENCE IN OUR PERCEPTION FOR PRECISE
FORMS MAY WELL HAVE DEEP ROOTS AND EXTEND
TO THE INSTINCTIVE LEVEL. LORENZ HAD THE BRILLIANT
INSIGHT THAT THE UNIVERSAL CHARACTERISTIC OF
THE RELEASING SIGNAL IS ITS IMPROBABILITY. THIS
HOLDS TRUE FOR THE CHEMICAL SIGNALS OF SMELL
AS WELL AS FOR ACOUSTICAL (SUCH AS THE COCK'S
CROWING) AND VISUAL ONES, IN WHICH REGULAR,
SYMMETRICAL FIGURES, RHYTHMIC PATTERNS OF MOVEMEN
AND COLORS PLAY A CRUCIAL ROLE. ALL OF THESE
PRECISE SIGNALS ARE IMPROBABLE IN THE SENSE THAT
THEY STAND OUT FROM THE CONFUSION OF THE
BACKGROUND OF TOTAL PERCEPTION AS BEING CONSPI-
CUOUS. BY THE SAME TOKEN, THE PROTECTIVE COLORIN
OF MANY ANIMALS, BY MEANS OF WHICH THEY RENDER
THEMSELVES INCONSPICUOUS, MEANS THAT THEY RELEGAT
THEMSELVES TO AN AVERAGE STATUS OR ZERO LEVEL
IN THEIR SURROUNDINGS; PALE OR SPOTTED PATTERNS ALONG
WITH GREY, BROWNISH, AND MUTED TONES PREDOMINATE WHIL
COLORS OF THE SPECTRUM ARE AVOIDED. ONE CAN ULTIMATEL
EXPLAIN THE PREFERENCE FOR SYMMETRICAL FIGURES
ONLY BY THEIR IMPROBABILITY.

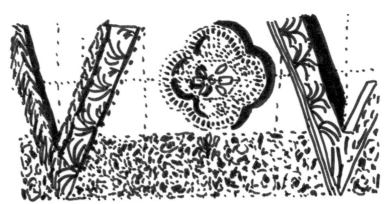

MSHATTA FAÇADE   VIII CENTURY
QASR MSHATTA · JORDAN

K. A. C. CRESWELL
1879 - 1974

CRESWELL, EARLY MUSLIM ARCHITECTURE
(VOLUME I 1932 - VOLUME II 1940)
SEE   ALSO (AND MAYBE BUY)

K. A. C. CRESWELL, A SHORT
ACCOUNT OF EARLY MUSLIM
ARCHITECTURE

"THE EVEN COVERING OF THE FIELD"

SANT'APOLLINARE NUOVO
REBUILT 561 UNDER JUSTINIAN

DAMASCUS GREAT MOSQUE
OLEG GRABAR, THE ART AND
ARCHITECTURE OF ISLAM 650-
1250 AD (2001)

THE HUMAN FIGURES DISAPPEAR
THE CONDITION IS
BACKGROUND / BACKGROUND
ONLY TREES REMAIN, FIGUR
ARE SUBSTITUTED BY
GENERIC BUILDINGS

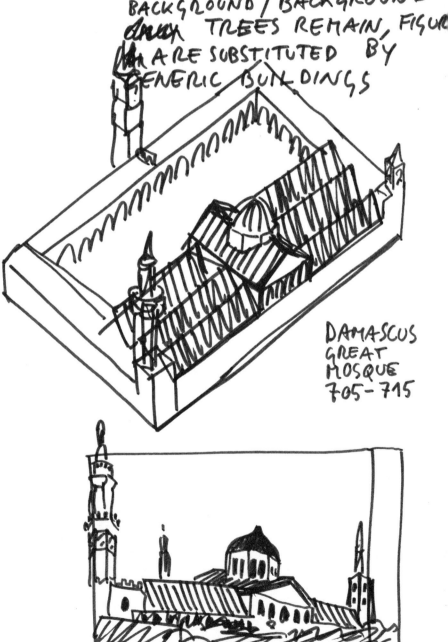

DAMASCUS
GREAT
MOSQUE
705-715

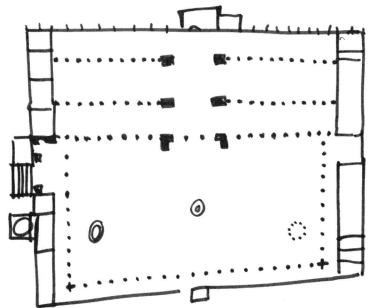

IT IS A CHRISTIAN
BASILICA TURNED 90°/
THIS BREAKS THE HYERARCHY
OF THE SPACE AND PRODUCES
AN INCREDIBLY EVEN, OPEN
CONDITION
BY SIMPLY INVERTING THE
AXES OF ACCESS SPACE ACQUIRES
A COMPLETELY DIFFERENT
TONE.

SAMARRA
848-851

DESTROYED
1278

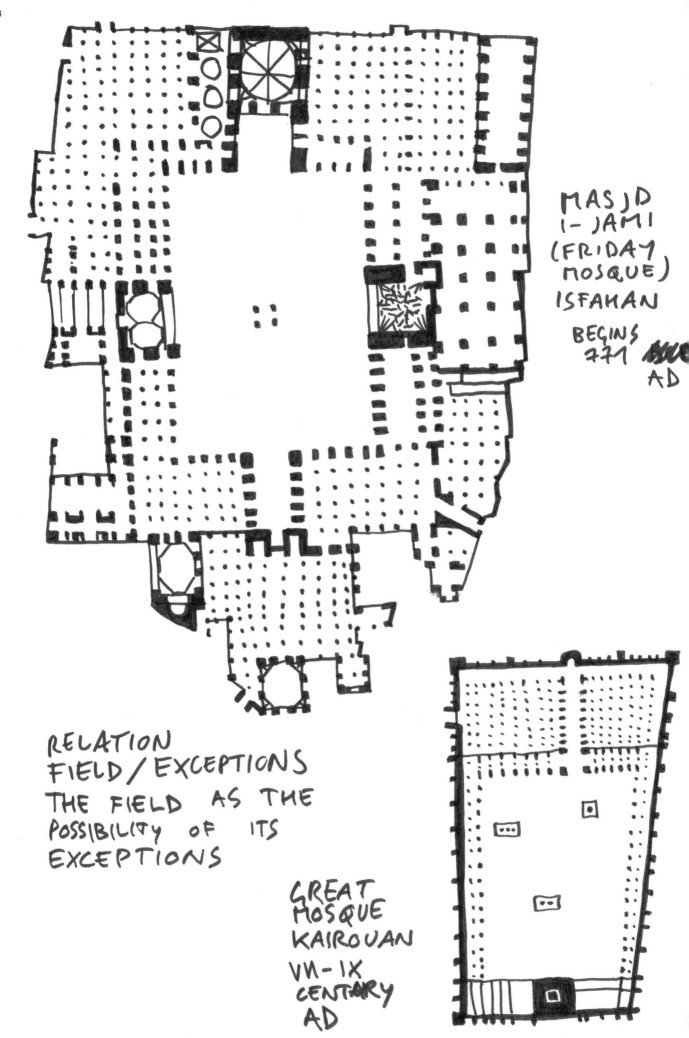

MASJD
I-JAMI
(FRIDAY
MOSQUE)
ISFAHAN

BEGINS
771
AD

RELATION
FIELD/EXCEPTIONS
THE FIELD AS THE
POSSIBILITY OF ITS
EXCEPTIONS

GREAT
MOSQUE
KAIROUAN

VII-IX
CENTURY
AD

KAIROUAN

MASJD I-JAMI ISFAHAN

IF WE LOOK AT THE FOUR
IWAN OF THE ISFAHAN
MOSQUE FROM THE POINT
OF VIEW OF VENTURI/SCOTT
BROWN (LERNING FROM LAS
VEGAS, 1972) IDEA THAT
ALL BUILDINGS ARE
EITHER :

DUCK

DECORATED
SHED

THE IWANS (COVERED IN TILES)
ARE LIKE THE DUCK CHOPPED
WITH THE DECORATED SHED

BELLY OF THE DUCK

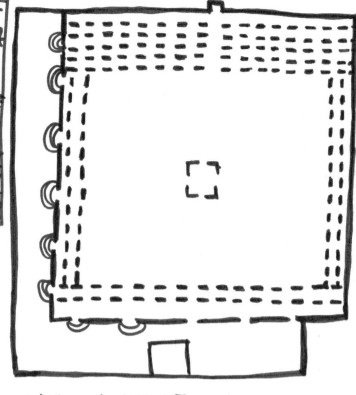

MOSQUE   IBN-TULUN
CAIRO   876-79

THE STORAGE-LIKE ATMOSPHERE
PRODUCED BY THE REPETITION OF
THE STURDY, SCARCELY DECORATED
RECTANGULAR PILLARS
CONFRONT SCHINKEL'S IDEA OF   IBN TULUN MOSQUE
THE CHURCH AS "STORAGE TO PREACH"

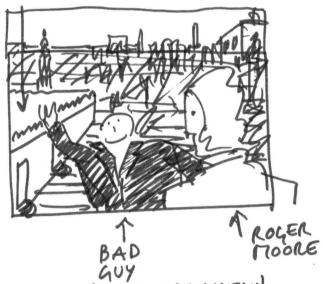

↑
BAD
GUY
(SOVIET, MOST LIKELY)

↑ ROGER
   MOORE

THE SPY WHO LOVED ME, 1977

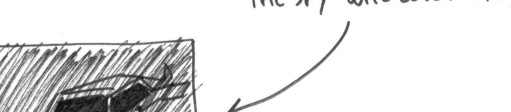

CORDOBA
MOSQUE

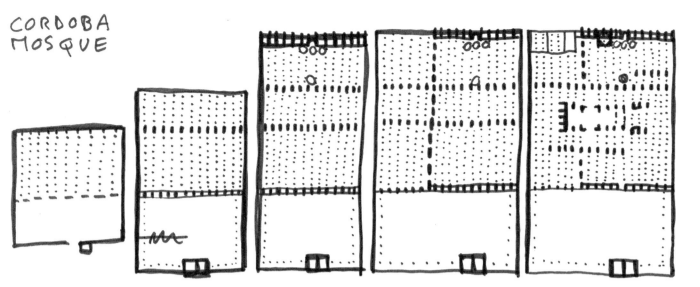

| ABD-AL-RAHMAN I 785 | ABD AL-RAHMAN II 833-848 | AL HAKAM II 961 | AL MANSOUR 987-988 | CAPILLA MAYOR 1523-1607 |

IT IS IMPORTANT TO NOTICE THAT ALSO THE CHRISTIAN
TRANSFORMATIONS, HOWEVER VIOLENT, FOLLOW THE PATTERN
ESTABLISHED BY THE MUSLIM BUILDERS.

SEE   R. MONEO, LA VIDA DE LOS EDIFICIOS, "ARQUITECTURE" 256
          1985, p. 27-36

     S. ALLEN, FIELD CONDITIONS IN ARCHITECTURE AND
          URBANISM, "THE BERLAGE PAPERS" 17, 1996

LE CORBUSIER ASSEMBLY
CHANDIGHAR 1951-1962

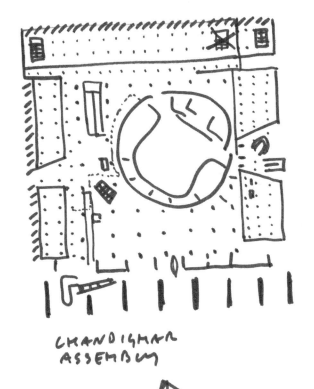

CHANDIGHAR
ASSEMBLY

OMA · AGADIR CONVENTION
CENTRE · 1990

THE FASCINATION FOR PLAIN
NON ARCHITECTURE (SOME OF
THE FREEDOM OF THE ERLY
MUSLIM, PURE BACKGROUND
ARCHITECTURE)
OMA IS FAR LESS "AUTHORIAC
TAAN CLASSIC MODERNISM

" ARCHITECTURE IS MONSTROUS IN THE WAY IN WHI
EACH CHOICE LEADS TO THE REDUCTION OF
POSSIBILITY " R. KOOLHAAS, TYPICAL PLAN, 1993

LUDWIG HILBERSEIMER
1885 - 1967

HILBERSEIMER
CHICAGO
TRIBUNE
1922

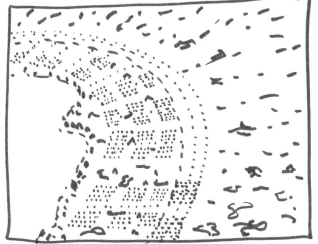

LUDWIG HILBERSEIMER / ALFRED
CALDWELL - STUDIES FOR
CHICAGO AREA · 1942

The same desire for architecture
to disappear into social
infrastructure
YET THE EXTREMERADICALISM
OF THIS ACT OF DISAPPEARANCE
TURNS OUT INTO A SORT OF
AESTHETIC OF ITS OWN

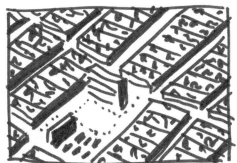

IRENEO
DIOTALLEVI
FRANCO
MARESCOTTI

CITTÀ
ORIZZONTALE

1940

THE AMBITION FOR AN ARCHITECTURE WITHOUT FIGURE, SIMPLY
PROVIDING SPATIAL "SERVICES"

ADALBERTO LIBERA
TUSCOLANO 1950-54
ROMA

THE RADICALISM OF HILBERSEIM
OR MARESCOTTI/DIOTALLEVI FINDS
SOMEHOW MILDER, MORE TOLERA
INTERPRETATION

J.P. OUD KIEFHOEK
ROTTERDAM 1925-30

HILBERSEIMER
FRIEDRICHSTADT 1928

MIES VAN DER ROHE
REICHSBANK 1933

WHILE MORE AMBITIOUS, MORE
FORMALLY "RELEVANT", THE
REICHSBANK IS ALSO MORE
CONTEXTUAL, MORE ADAPTED
TO CIRCUMSTANCES, AND SO
DISAPPEARS INTO BACKGROUND
MORE THAN OSTENTATIOUSLY
HUBLE DESIGN OF HILBERSEIMER

PERRAULT

LOUVRE

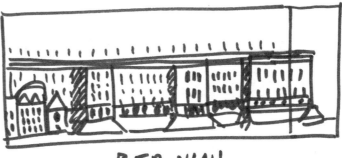

BERNINI
(RIVER FAÇADE)

REICHSBANK

142

FRIEDRICHSTRASSE
TOWER
VERSION 1922

REICHSBANK
1933

BUT THERE IS ALSO A MUCH
MORE FIGURATIVE VERSION
OF MIES

NORMAN FOSTER
WILLIS FABER DUMAS
IPSWICH 1975

MIES INVISIBLE SHAPES
AMERICAN +CORPORATE OFFICES
=
A LIGHT POP NEW WORLD

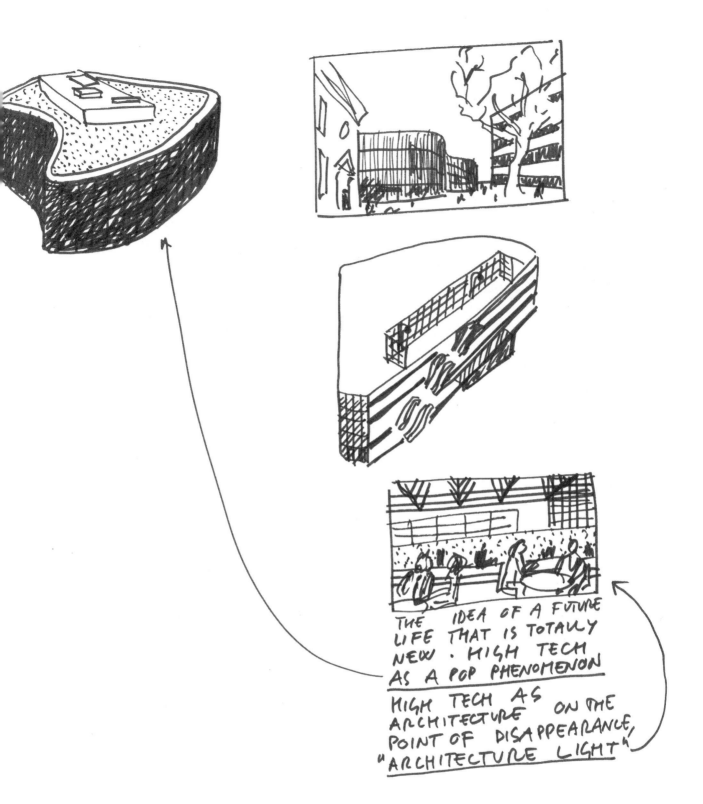

THE IDEA OF A FUTURE
LIFE THAT IS TOTALLY
NEW. HIGH TECH
AS A POP PHENOMENON

HIGH TECH AS
ARCHITECTURE ON THE
POINT OF DISAPPEARANCE,
"ARCHITECTURE LIGHT"

RAFFAELE STERN
RESTORATION COLISEUM
EASTERN BUTTRESS
1806-07

GIUSEPPE VALADIER
RESTORATION COLISEUM
WESTERN BUTTRESS
1823-26

CONTINUITY IS NO
MORE POSSIBLE /
FORMS MUST BE
RADICALLY DIFFERENT
FROM THE PAST

CONTINUITY IS POSSIBLE
FORMS CAN FIND A
NEW NON-CONFLICTUAL
RELATION WITH THE
PAST
(THE MOST TRADITIONALIST
OF THE TWO RESTORATION.
IS THE MOST RECENT)

HANS DÖLLGAST
RESTORATION ALTE
PINAKOTHEK MÜNCHEN
1952-57

THE LIBRARY (1989!)
OES NOT TAKE THE CRITICAL
TAND TOWARDS THE SUBDIVISION
F LAND IN THE CAPITALIST CITY
HAT WAS THE REASON FOR
HE AWKWARD (AND AMAZINGLY
EAUTIFUL) RHYTM OF THE
RIESTE PROJECT

GIORGIO
GRASSI
PUBLIC
LIBRARY
GRONINGEN
1989

LASSI. ~~OANSS DOUD CSOBOBTE~~
E HEADQUARTERS REGION
RIESTE 1974

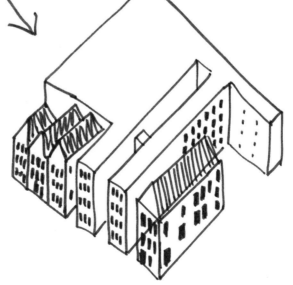

THE LIBRARY DISAPPEARS
IN ITS CONTEXT EMERGING
SIMPLY AS A SORT OF
COMMENTARY ON THE
EXISTING CITY

146

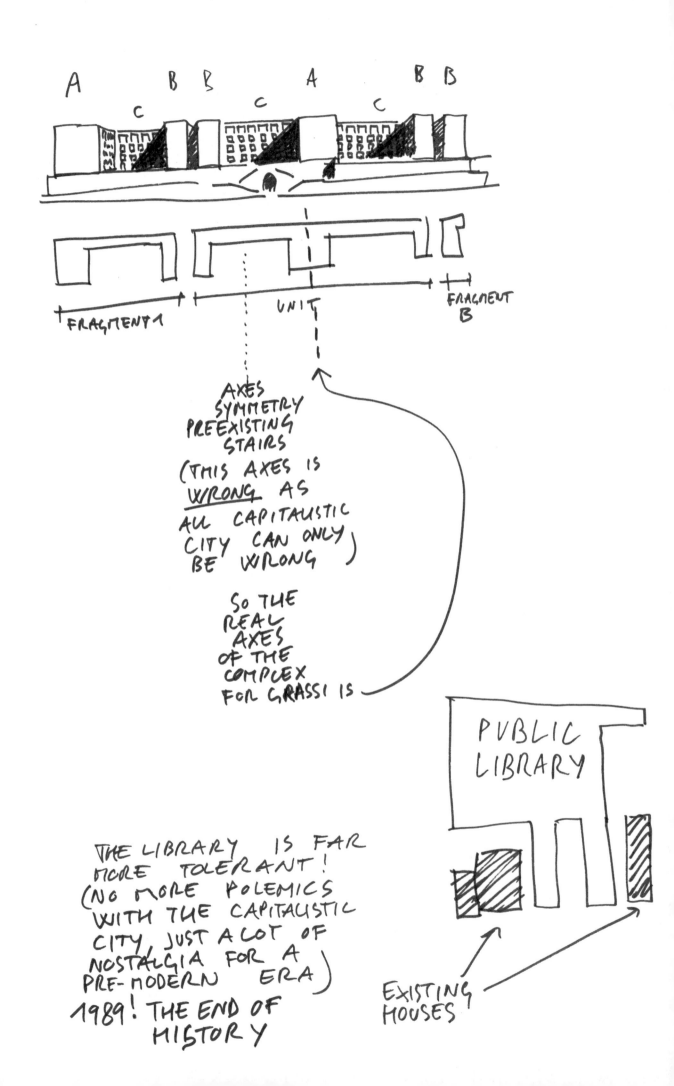

A   B   B   A   B   B

C   C   C

FRAGMENT 1   UNIT   FRAGMENT B

AXES
SYMMETRY
PREEXISTING
STAIRS
(THIS AXES IS
WRONG AS
ALL CAPITALISTIC
CITY CAN ONLY)
BE WRONG

SO THE
REAL
AXES
OF THE
COMPLEX
FOR GRASSI IS

PUBLIC
LIBRARY

THE LIBRARY IS FAR
MORE TOLERANT!
(NO MORE POLEMICS
WITH THE CAPITALISTIC
CITY, JUST A LOT OF
NOSTALGIA FOR A
PRE-MODERN ERA)
1989! THE END OF
HISTORY

EXISTING
HOUSES

GIORGIO MORANDI
STILL LIFE 1956

F.O. GHERY INDIANA
AVENUE STUDIOS 1981

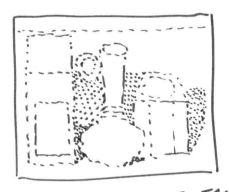

THE EXTREME MONUMENTALITY
OF THE VERY BANAL BOTTLES
AND BOWELS BY MORANDI

"THE GRAND FIGURES,
THE GRAND ACTION,
AND THE SEVERE
LANDSCAPE"

B. BERENSON ON
PIERO DELLA FRANCESCA
THE ITALIAN PAINTERS
OF THE RENAISSANCE, 1952

GHERY'S COMPOSITION MAKES
EXPLICIT REFERENCE TO
MORANDI, BUT REMAINS
MUCH MORE MODEST. THERE
IS NO "GRAND FIGURES" HERE

PHILIP GUSTON DRAWING 1960s

P. GUSTON   ROME 1977
(GUSTON IN ROME 1970-71)
GUSTON UNHAPPY WITH
ABSTRACT EXPRESSIONISM
GOES ROME

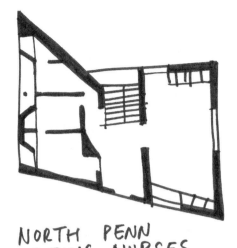

NORTH PENN
VISITING NURSES
ASSOCIATION 1961
ROBERT VENTURI

(ROBERT VENTURI IN ROME
1954)
VENTURI UNHAPPY
WITH MODERNISM GOES
ROME

GUSTON   RED BOX 1977

ALIGHIERO BOETTI 197

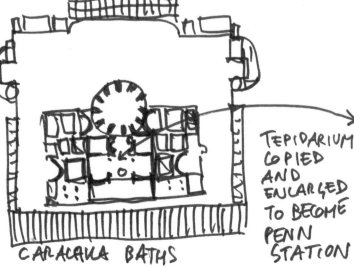

CARACALLA BATHS

TEPIDARIUM
COPIED
AND
ENLARGED
TO BECOME
PENN
STATION

PENN STATION REMAINS EXTREMELY LOW. MCKIM REFUSES TO ADD TOWER. THE BUILDING AS ICON VANISHES AND OPERATES AS PUBLIC SPACE JUST AS A COLOSSAL INTERIOR.

MOPS   COURT   TEPIDARIUM
   FRIGIDARIUM   CALIDRIUM

PENN STATION WAS DEMOLISHED IN 1963

PENN STATION MELTING INTO CITY FABRIC - COPY AS A DEVICE FOR ARCHITECTURE TO

SEE ALSO COPY OF PALAZZO GRIMANI FOR TIFFANY

RIMANI 1556   TIFFANY 1903

DISAPPEAR

ECLECTICISM / CLASSICISM

VIII

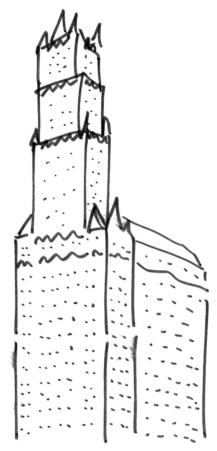

CASS GILBERT 1913
WOOLWORTH BUILDING
(UNTIL 1930 TALLEST)
BUILDING IN THE WORLD

K.F. SCHINKEL 1824-
FRIEDRICH SCHWERDERSCHE K

" I LIKE TO DEVELOP A
SUBJECT IN THE STYLE WHICH
SEEMS BEST ADAPTED TO THE
PURPOSE "
(CASS GILBERT TO GEORGE DUDLEY
SEYMOUR 30/10/1908)

" I AM IN FACT,
COMPLETELY
OPPOSED TO THE
IDEA THAT A SPECIFI
BUILDING SHOULD
HAVE AN INDIVIDUAL
CHARACHTER "

(MIES VAN DER ROHE TO MSSR
CAMERON ALREAD, EDOW DAVID
EDGAR MARSHALL, LOUIS THOMAS,
11/05/1960)

ECLECTICISM AS THE USE OF ALL REPERTOIR
BECAUSE THEY ARE DIFFERENT / CLASSICISM
AS THE USE OF ALL REPERTOIRES BECAUSE THEY ARE
THE SAME

ECLECTICISM PRESUPPOSES SAMENESS AND SEARCHES
VARIETY — CLASSICISM PRESUPPOSES COMPLEXITY
AND LOOKS FOR CLARITY

(FORGET "EDLE EINFALT")

FOR ECLECTICISM, REALITY IS BORING AND
WE MUST FIND SOMETHING NEW: ARCHITECTURE
MUST BECOME FICTION
FOR CLASSICISM REALITY IS ENOUGH; THERE
IS NOTHING TO INVENT

NEC FLERE, NEC INDIGNARI,
SED INTELLIGERE

ALL
BLUE

THE "BLUE PERIOD"

PICASSO, TWO WOMAN
AT A BAR, 1902

RED SPOTS

ALL
BLUE

THIS
RED

RICHTER, ABSTRACT
PAINTING   1999

"PAINTING WAS MY ATTEMPT TO
EXPLORE WHAT PAINTING IS STILL
ABLE AND PERMITTED TO DO"
RICHTER
1984

BROWN
GREY

THE "PINK PERIOD"

PICASSO, BOY LEADING
A HORSE, 1906

ALL
GREY

RICHTER, MOTOR BOOT
1965

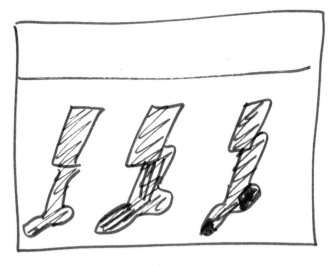

A. WHAROL
CAMPBELL SOUP

S. POLKE
SOCKEN, 1963

"DEMONSTRATION FOR
CAPITALIST REALISM"
(DÜSSELDORF 1963)

POLKE AND RICHTER
BOTH STUDIED
"SOCIALIST REALISM
IN THE DDR

SEE ALSO
MARK FISHER, CAPITALIST REALISM:
IS THERE NO ALTERNATIV
2009

FOR RICHTER AND POLKE
THE ACT OF REPRODUCTION
IS INDIFFERENT TO CONTENT
FOR WHAROL THE ACT OF
REPRODUCTION COINCIDES
WITH THE SELECTION OF
CONTENT

CLASSIC ART HAS NO CONT
OR BETTER; CONTENT IS
NEVER AN ISSUE FOR CLASSI
ART

ROY LICHTENSTEIN
WHAAM! 1963

GERHARD RICHTER
DÜSENJÄGER 1963

"FOR ME THERE'S NO DIFFERENCE
BETWEEN A LANDSCAPE AND
AN ABSTRACT PAINTING"
RICHTER 1973

"IN VENICE THERE IS AN INTERNATIONAL
EXHIBITION WITH A THEME: REALITY
AND ABSTRACTION, IN TWO SEPARATE
PAVILIONS. I SENT TWO IDENTICAL
LARGE MONOCHROME GREY PAINTINGS
AND THEY PUT ONE IN THE REALIST
PAVILION AND ONE IN THE ABSTRACT
PAVILION" RICHTER 1978
↓
G. RICHTER, WRITINGS
1961-2007, NEW YORK, DAP
2009

IF STYLE CORRESPONDS
TO CONTENT (OR FORM
CORRESPONDS TO FUNCTION),
THEN STYLE (OR FORM)
WILL HAVE TO CHANGE
ACCORDING TO CONTENT (FUNCTION)

THIS IS ALSO WHY
ECLECTICISM LED
TO MODERNISM

STYLE CORRESPONDS
TO CONTENT
VS
ALL STYLES CAN BE
MIXED TO ADAPT TO CONTENT

MANTEGNA, TRIONFI DI
CESARE, 1484-92

RAPHAEL'S
CAPACITY
TO
LEARN
FROM
ANYONE

(HERE
FROM
MICHEL-
ANGELO)

RAPHAEL, THE FIRE AT
BORGO, 1514-17

PARKER BRIGHT
STANDING IN FRONT
OF DANA SCHUTZ'S PAINTING
"OPEN CASKET" AT WHITNEY
BIENNALE, NEW YORK, 2016

ONLY CERTAIN IDENTITY
GROUPS CAN ELABORATE
ADDRESS CERTAIN SUBJECTS
IS IDENTITY-BASED ART
A FORM OF ECLECTISM?

DANA SCHUTZ
OPEN CASKET, 2016
(EMMETT TILL'S BODY)
IN A CASKET

EVERYONE IS
ALLOWED TO
PAINT (OR PRODUCE
ART ABOUT) ANY
CONTENT

GENERAL CONDITIONS
FOR PRODUCING ART
ACCORDING TO ENZO
MARI 1986 ⟶

① PHYDIAS - I, NON-SUBJECTIVELY REPRESENT THE IDEA OF THE SACRED
② GALILEO - I DENY REPRESENTATION AND NON-SUBJECTIVELY TRY TO EXPLAIN NATURE
③ DUCHAMP - I SUBJECTIVELY DENY ANYONE WHO STILL REPRESENT THE IDEA OF THE SACRED
④ SEVEN DWARVES - WE, TODAY, SUBJECTIVELY REPRESENT IN THE ABSENCE OF ANY IDEA
⑤ THE IDIOT - WE NEED A NON SUBJECTIVE IDEA OF NATURE - GOD

Enzo Mari, Dialogue among Phidias, Galileo, Duchamp, 7 dwarves

K. F. SCHINKEL · FRIEDRICHSWERDERSCHE KIRCHE 1824 - FOUR VERSIONS

SCHINKEL PRESENTED FOUR DIFFERENT VERSIONS TO THE KING

STYLE IS DIFFERENT BUT RELATION OF THE BOX TO THE CITY IS ALWAYS THE SAME

FRIEDRICHSWERDERSCHE KIRCHE 1824 - 30

STILL THE INTERIOR IS DIFFERENT

THE "CLASSIC" VERSION IS MORE CEREMONIAL MOVEMENT IS SOMEHOW SLOWER

THE "GOTHIC" VERSION IS MORE UNIDIRECTIONAL AND TIGHT

THE ELEGANCE OF THE
MINOR SHIFT IN THE
POSITION OF THE
CHURCH IN THE
URBAN CONTEXT

THE BRICK BOX
SLIDES IN THE
HAVELLANDSCHAFT
SCHINKEL'S CAPACITY
TO READ THE GEOLOGICA
CONDITION OF BERLIN

THE ~~DORIC~~ GIGANTIC DORIC
COLUMN WAS AN ANSWER
TO A REQUEST FOR THE
"MOST BEAUTIFUL AND
DISTINCTIVE OFFICE BUILDING
IN THE WORLD"

A SERIOUS (DAMN SERIOUS, AND
ABIT STUPID) APPROACH TO
MONUMENTALITY   IS
J.L. SERT, F. LÉGER, S. GIEDION
NINE POINTS ON MONUMENTALITY
    1943

ADOLF
LOOS
CHICAGO
TRIBUNE
PROPOSAL
1922

LOOS SHOWS SAME
INDIFFERENCE TO
STYLE OF SCHINKEL
(OR MMSVW) BUT
IN A FEROCIOUSLY SARCASTIC

FERNAND LÉGER 1942
LES PLONGEURS

LÉGER'S ATTEMPTS TO
PRODUCE ONCE AGAIN
PUBLIC-POLITICAL ART
(MONUMENTAL MURAL
PAINTING) TRYING TO
RECONNECT AVANT-GARDE
TO A POLITICAL COMMITMENT
    SEE RIVERA'S ATTEMPTS
    AT COMMUNIST MURALES

MONUMENTALITY THROUGH
INDIFFERENCE TO
CONTENT
MIES VAN DER ROHE
DOMINION CENTRE
TORONTO   1967

LÉGER'S PLONGEURS
IN W.K. HARRISON'S
LIVING ROOM   TROTSKY

THE PAINTING WAS RENDUED

MARX

AIL

SION
D IN
XICO
REPAINTED

VERA DIEGO RIVERA, MAN AT A CROSSROAD, ROCKFELLER CENTRE, 1934

STANLEY TIGERMAN
BLACK BARN 1973-74
FRESH HOLLOW MICHIGAN

JAMES STIRLING
CAMBRIDGE HISTORY LIBRA...
1963-68

OBSERVING THE ARCHITECTURE
OF THE PAST IN SEARCH
FOR A THEME / OBSERVING THE
ARCHITECTURE OF
THE PAST IN SEARC...
FOR FORMAL LAWS

THIS IS MIES
CROWN HALL
AT IIT CAMPUS

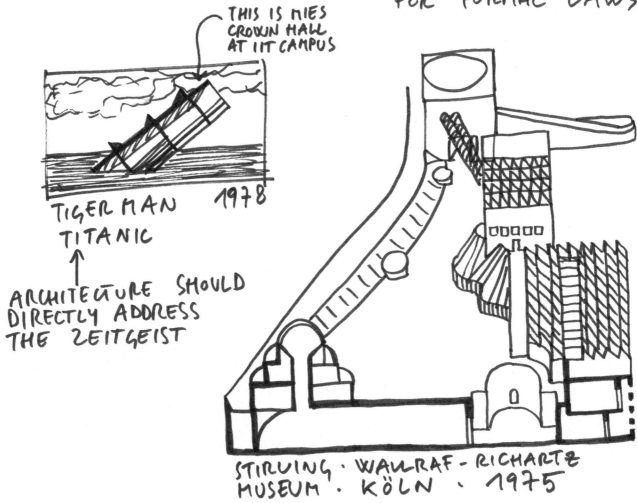

TIGERMAN 1978
TITANIC
↑
ARCHITECTURE SHOULD
DIRECTLY ADDRESS
THE ZEITGEIST

STIRLING · WALRAF-RICHARTZ
MUSEUM · KÖLN · 1975

TIGERMAN, HOT DOG HOUSE
HARVARD, ILLINOIS, 1972-74

OASE 79: THE ARCHITECTURE
OF JAMES STIRLING
1964-1992: A NON-DOGMATIC
ACCUMULATION OF FORMAL
KNOWLEDGE

STIRLING · BIENNALE BOOKSHOP 1991
VENICE

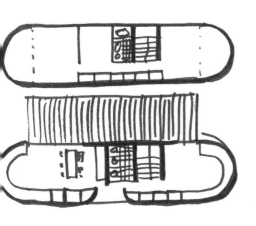

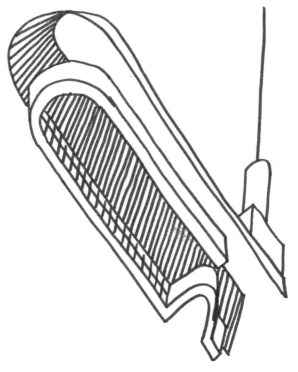

PALLADIO · VILLA SEREGO
1560-70

PALLADIO TREATS RURAL
ARCHITECTURE AS SOMETHING
DIFFERENT FROM METROPOLITAN
ARCHITECTURE / RURAL AND
URBAN SPLIT ROLES LIKE
LATIN AND VERNACULAR :
THERE ARE HIGH, METROPOLITAN
(LATIN) SUBJECTS AND LOW,
RURAL (VERNACULAR) SUBJECTS

"SANSOVINO'S VILLA IN PONTECAS
[...] WAS SOMETHING APART. AW
IN THE ADIGE DELTA, SOAKED E
RAIN AND FOG AND BATTERED E
SUN, IT REPRESENTED A BEAUT
ABERRATION IN THE EVOLUTIO
OF ARCHITECTURE THAT WAS TO
HAVE NO PROGENY. SANSOVINO
ENVISAGED THE COUNTRY VILLA T
HE BUILT FOR THE GARZONI FAMI
IN THE LATER 1540S AS A RUR
PALACE OF NOBLE DIMENSIONS.
LIKE THE OTHER VILLAS IN TH
VENETIAN TRADITION, IT HAS T
FAMILIAR CENTRAL LOGGIA AND
SIDE BLOCKS, BUT IT IS SOMEHO
TOO AULIC FOR THE COUNTRY,
LIKE A DOGE AT A SWIMMING
HOLE" J. S. ACKERMAN, PALLA

JACOPO SANSOVINO 1540
VILLA GARZONI PONTECASAL
NO RURAL ATMOSPHERE
HERE

PALAZZO ZUCCARI
1590 - 1610

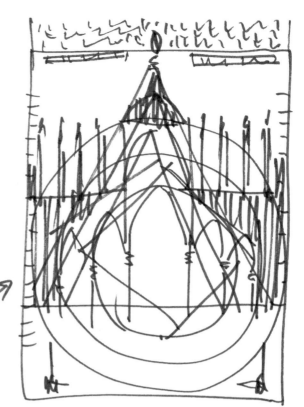

CESARIANO, MILAN
CATHEDRAL, ILLUSTRATION
FOR THE ITALIAN TRANSLATION
OF VITRUVIUS, COMO 1521

CESARIANO
PUTS A GOTHIC
CATHEDRAL IN
HIS VITRUVIUS.
HE IS PROBABLY
INFLUENCED BY
BRAMANTE'S
INTERPRETATION
OF THE CATHEDRAL
AS IN HIS REPORT
("OPINIO") ON THE
DOME CA. 1490

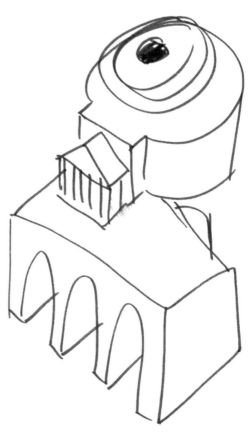

BRAMANTE'S
ST. PETER'S AS
PANTHEON
+
BASILICA
NO NEED FOR
INVENTION, NO SYMBOLISM. THE MOST
IMPORTANT CHURCH IS TO BE TREATED AS
ANY OTHER CHURCH, JUST BIGGER.

ANTONIO DA SANGALLO TH[E]
YOUNGER FOR BRAMANT[E]
CAPITAL OF ST. PETER'S
CA. 1507

BRAMANTE SENDS ANTON[IO]
TO THE PANTHEON TO
COPY THE CAPITAL (OF T[HE]
PILASTER IN THE PORTICO[)]
AS HE ADVICED 25 YEARS
BEFORE WHEN ASKED ABO[UT]
ORNAMENT FOR THE MIL[AN]
CATHEDRAL, BRAMANTE
SIMPLY PROPOSES TO
COPY WHAT IS ALREA[DY]
THERE.

BRAMANTE CORRECTS GIULIANO

GIULIANO DA
SANGALLO U8AR

BRAMANTE USES MANY
REPERTOIRES BUT HE DOES
NOT SHOW THEM

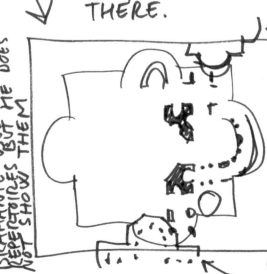

QUOT[E]
SAN
LORE[NZO]
MIL[AN]

BRAMAN[TE]
U8A[R]

QUOTE MIL[AN]
CATHEDRA[L]

JACOPO BAROZZI DA VIGNOLA 1565-68

THE PERFECT HUMBLENESS
OF THE PORTICO DEI BANCHI
NO STYLISTIC ADAPTATION TO
CONTEXT, JUST THE PERFECT
MEASUREMENTS, THE CAPACITY
TO RECOGNIZE AND ADAPT, TO
INTEGRATE EXCEPTIONS

S. ANDREA ALLA VIA
FLAMINIA   1553

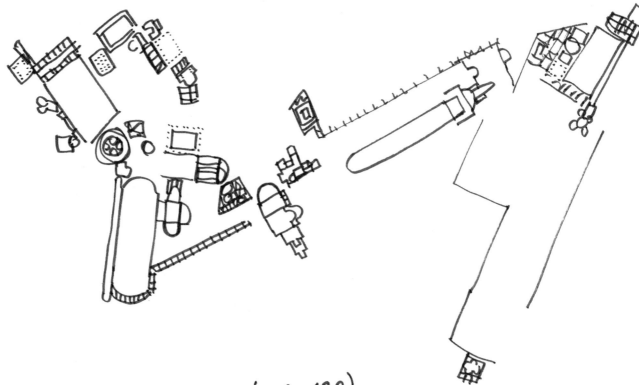

VILLA ADRIANA (118-138)
THE DIFFERENT BUILDINGS AS RECREATION OF
PLACES OF THE EMPIRE

"CANOPUS", VILLA ADRIANA
THE RECREATION OF
AN EGYPTIAN LANDSCAPE
(THE CITY AND CANAL OF
CANOPUS IN THE WESTERN
PART OF THE NILE DELTA)

ARCHITECTURE AS
A COLLECTION OF
MEMORIES

MIES VAN DER ROHE
VILLA TUGENDHAT
BRNO. 1929-30

ARCHITECTURE AS
A MACHINE TO
ACTIVATE MEMORIES

SALVADOR DALÍ
HOUSE IN PORTLLIGAT
1930-1982
ARCHITECTURE AS
AUTOBIOGRAPHICAL
NARRATION

ARCHITECTURE AS NARRATION,
AS ESCAPE, AS THERAPY?

HANS HOLLEIN 1978-79
TRAVEL AGENCY

THE
CASTLE
AS A
PHANTASY
AS A TOOL
TO GO
BACK IN
TIME

SCHLOSS NEUSCHWANSTEIN
1868-1882 ARCHITECT
EDUARD RIEDL, IN COLLABORATION
WITH STAGE DESIGNER CHRISTIAN JANK

THE
CASTLE
AS RATIONAL
MILITARY
INFRASTRUC-
TURE AND
AS A
PROJECT
OF CONTROL
OF NATURE
AND
SOCIETY

CASTEL DEL MONTE
CA. 1240

CLASSICISM AS AN ARCHITECTURE
OF CONQUEST/ECLECTICISM AS
THE ARCHITECTURE OF A CONQUERED
WORLD

168

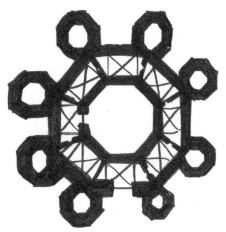

CARLO MOLLINO
RECONSTRUCTION TEATRO
REGIO · TORINO 1965-73

AN ARCHITECTURE THAT
TRIES TO ENVISION ANOTHER
WORLD

CASTEL DEL
MONTE CA.1240

AN ARCHITECTURE
OF REALITY (OF
UNDERSTANDING AND
CONTROL OVER REALITY)

LEON KRIER · ATLANTIS
(TENERIFE · 1986)

A NOSTALGIC/REGRESSIVE
UTOPIA

JOHN NASH · ROYAL
PAVILION BRIGHTON 1827

AN INDIFFERENT, SARCA-
FORMAL INVESTIGATION

K.F. SCHINKEL
ZELTZIMMER
POTSDAM
1826-29

A FAKE TENT INSIDE A ROYAL
FOR THE PRINCE TRAINING THE A

BORIS IOFAN · MOSKOW STATE
UNIVERSITY 1947

A DUMB BUT VERBOSE EXPRESSION
OF POWER · AN ATTEMPT AT
COMMUNICATING INCREDIBLY
CRUDE AND VIOLENT MESSAGES

G. GRASSI
BIBLIOTECA
PORTA VOLTA
MILANO 1990

AN EXPLICIT REFUSAL
OF ANY COMMUNICATION
"ARCHITECTURE DEAD
    LANGUAGE"
THE BUILDING AS AN OBSTACLE
INSIDE THE CITY; THE
BUILDING AS SOMETHING
ACTING BY BEING AVOIDED

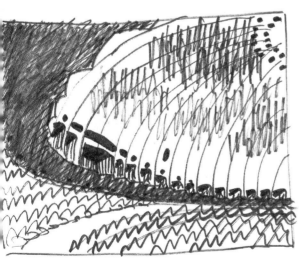

MOLLING · TEATRO REGIO

ECLECTIC / EXOTIC
SPECTACLE

THE FALL OF THE ROMAN
EMPIRE 1964

CLASSIC / POPULAR
SPECTACLE
CLASSIC ROME ⟷ HOLLYWOOD
            McLUHAN, GUTENBERG

GALAXY 1962

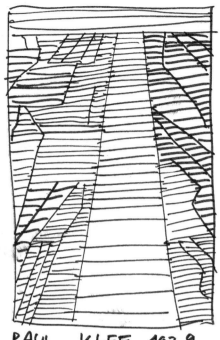

PAUL KLEE 1929
HIGHWAY AND BYWAYS

ILYA REPIN, COSSACKS WRITE A
LETTER TO THE TURKISH SULTAN
1880-91

AVANT-GARDE ART
DELIBERATELY TRIES
TO SPLIT THE AUDIENCE
AMONG SUPPORTERS AND
ADVERSARIES ISOLATE
"CONOISSEURS"

AUERBACH ON AUERBACH,
GONCOURTS' MIMESIS,
GERMINIE LACERTEUX 1946,

CLEMENT GREENBERG,
AVANT-GARDE AND KITSCH
"PARTISAN REVIEW", 1939

"ALL KITSCH IS ACADEMIC, AND
CONVERSELY, ALL THAT IS
ACADEMIC IS KITSCH"

AVANT-GARDE
AND DISTINCTION
P. BOURDIEU, LA DISTINCTION,
CRITIQUE SOCIALE DU JUGEMENT
1979 (ENGLISH: DISTINCTION: A
SOCIAL CRITIQUE OF THE JUDGEMENT
OF TASTE, 1984)

SEE HANNES MEYER
ON THE REASONS
OF THE "CLASSICAL
SEE: V.PAPERNY, TURN" IN STALINIST
CULTURE USSR
TWO. ARCHITECTURE
IN THE AGE OF
STALIN, 2011

AN EXPLICIT ATTEMPT OF POST-
REVOLUTIONARY RUSSIAN ELITES
TO ABANDON AVANT-GARDE
AND REAPPROPRIATE A POPULAR
FORM OF ART

BOLSHEVIKS WRITING LETTER
TO LORD CURZON
THE CARTOON INCLUDES ALL
SOVIET LEADERS: KAMENEV, BUKH
TROTSKY, STALIN, ZINONIEV
EXPLICITLY REFERS TO
REPIN'S KITSCH PAINTING

THE LADDER
IN THE
PHOTO
IS A PART
OF THE
MONUMENT

VLADIMIR TATLIN, MONUMENT
TO THE THIRD INTERNATIONAL
1919-20

TATLIN'S MONUMENT AS AN ATTEMPT
TO ~~RECOVER~~ RECOVER "HIGH TECH"
FROM THE PETTY DREAMS OF THE
BOURGEOISIE TO PUT THEM AT
THE SERVICE OF THE WORKING
CLASS. TATLIN'S TOWER IS A
RE-MAKE OF THE TOUR EIFFEL
FROM "THE POINT OF VIEW OF
TOTALITY" (~~GEORGE~~ LUKÁCS)

THE IDEA OF A NEW UNIVERSALISM
OF THE PROLETARIAT APPEARS
BOTH IN SOME AVANT-GARDE
PROJECTS (SUCH AS TATLIN'S) AS
IN SOME STALINIST KITSCH

THERE IS A
KITSCH VERSION
OF CLASSICISM
BECAUSE CLASSICISM
WAS KITSCH ON
ITS OWN, SEE
ROMAN ARCHITECTURE

172

WERNER TÜBKE BAUERNKRIEGSPANORA
BAD FRANKENHAUSEN 1976-87
THE PAINTING IS 14×123 m
IS SIZE AN ELEMENT OF BEAUTY?
THE PROBLEMS ADDRESSED BY ART
IN A SOCIALIST SOCIETY WERE DIFFER

TÜBKE BAUERNKRIEGS-
PANORAMA DETAIL
1976-87

CLASSICAL GOALS
WITHOUT CLASSICAL
MEANS

RICHTER · KUH · 1964
CLASSICAL MEANS
WITHOUT CLASSICAL
GOALS

SALVADOR DALÍ
COLOSSUS OF RHODES
1956

PAINTED FOR A
HOLLYWOOD MOVIE
"THE SEVEN WONDERS
OF THE WORLD"
1956

TÜBKE   HONECKER
02-10-1982

AN ART THAT DOES NOT REFUSE
AN EVIDENT RELATION TO
POWER, DOESN'T REFUSE
TO ENTERTAIN
HOLLYWOOD, SOCIALIST REALISM,
CLASSIC ROME
    SEE DIALOGUE VERGIL/
AUGUSTUS IN HERMANN
BROCH'S VERGILS TOD

THE MARRIAGE OF
SALVADOR DALÍ AND
LE CORBUSIER ?

EE R. KOOLHAAS
LIRIOUS NEW YORK
DALÍ AND
ORBUSIER,
HAPTER V

DALÍ'S
CRUTCHES?

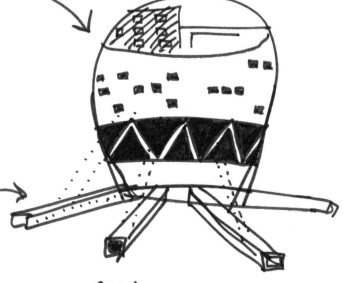

OMA   ZEEBRUGGE
1988

MA'S "GRAND PROJECTS" AS A
NTEMPORARY ATTEMPT TO COMBINE POPULAR IMAGERY
ITH CLASSICAL MEASURE

THE DIFFERENT
SOURCES USED
TO DEFINE THE
BUILDING
MERGE INTO
A NEW
OBJECT

PROPORTIONS
ARE WRONG,
MORE LIKE
HERE →

OMA, ZEEBRUGGE
TERMINAL 1988

☒ PART ADDED
BY BRAMANTE
TO CONSOLIDATE
THE BUILDING

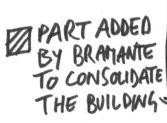

SACELLO DI SAN SATIRO
RESTORED 1490S (BRAMANTE)

THE PAVILION IS LIKE
A TINY TOWER MADE OF
GEOMETRIC PIECES ONE ON TOP
OF THE OTHER. THE ASSEMBLA
USES MANY PIECES TO PRODUCE A SING
OBJECT.

TIGERMAN
ILLINOIS REGIONAL LIBRARY
FOR THE BLIND AND PHISICALLY
HANDICAPPED, CHICAGO
1978

STIRLING   STAATSGALERIE
1977 - 84

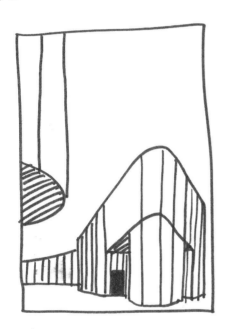

GUNNAR BIRKERTS
DULUTH PUBLIC LIBRARY
1980

CLASSICISM IS THE
USE OF ALL STYLES AS
IF THEY WERE ALL
EQUAL · CLASSICISM
IS INDIFFERENCE
TO STYLE

What is Architecture About? Eight Notes on the *Grundkurs* / Mark Lee

1. On the *Grundkurs*

The *Grundkurs* in architecture draws an outline of the foundations, rules, history, language, pace, process, and position of the discipline. Most importantly, it demarcates the first set of disciplinary boundaries.

Defining architecture entails making decisions on what architecture is and is not about. On one level, it is an act of disciplinary apartheid, building new walls (and consequently new slums) to separate what's in from what's out. On another level, this act of segregation promotes something that is often imperative in the formative stages of an education—a form of disciplinary autonomy.

Pier Paolo Tamburelli's *Grundkurs* draws the discipline's boundaries through eight lessons summarized as eight chapters in this book. Though there are examples from the fine arts, film, and design, its primary focus is always architecture. It defines clear and solid boundaries while offering limited external points of reference. In doing so, it serves notice that the aim here is to produce architecture, not sociology.

Disciplinary autonomy does not mean martial law: it does not have to last forever and does not equate to xenophobia. Imposed at the outset of one's education, it ensures much greater freedom down the road: "a dictatorship at the door and a democracy inside," is how Andy Warhol described this in relation to Studio 54.

2. On foundations

François Truffaut wrote that the entire career of a director is already present in his first 150 feet of film. Jean-Luc Godard said that you need "a beginning, middle, and end, but not necessarily in that order."

The *Grundkurs* is critical as it signifies the beginning of an architectural education, when the foundations of a life-long vocation are laid. Out of these first encounters with the discipline emerge the values and the ethos that the architect has to wrestle with, pin down, as they continue to evolve and transform in line with the trajectory of their practice.

Although the *Grundkurs* is situated at the beginning, there is a history of institutions where it is foregrounded as the apotheosis of the entire curriculum, from the Bauhaus in Germany to IIT in Chicago to Cooper Union in New York. The importance placed on the *Grundkurs* in these model pedagogical programs acknowledges that the question "What is Architecture about?" is one that recurs throughout an entire career.

Former professional basketball sharpshooter and coach Chuck Person said of his coaching technique: "I teach footwork, I teach the foundation. Most mistakes are made in the beginning. You can fix the middle, you can fix the top, but once you get started, it's hard to fix down low."

3. On rules

The art critic Dave Hickey dedicated his career to confronting both the pleasures and the misery inflicted by rules.

"I can remember being buoyed up, as a youth, by reading about Jackson Pollock in a magazine and seeing photographs of him painting. I was heartened by the stupid little rule through which Pollock civilized his violence. *It's okay to drip paint,* Jackson said. The magazine seemed to acquiesce: *Yeah, Jackson's right,* it seemed to say, grudgingly, *Dripping paint is now within the rules.* Even so, I had the right to be shocked a few years later when I enrolled in a university and discovered that Pollock's joyous permission had been translated into a prohibitive, institutional edict: *It's bad not to drip!* The art coaches said. *It means you got no soul!* Yikes!"

Hickey surmised: "the liberating rule that civilized us yesterday will, almost inevitably, seek to govern us tomorrow."

Are there rules imparted in the eight lessons outlined by Tamburelli's *Grundkurs*? And are they by nature liberating or governing? Tamburelli seems to know too well that while rules might change their operative purposes over time, they are not negotiable—but policies always are. By setting up dialectic couples for each lesson—Architecture / City, Roof / Wall, Figure / Ground, Profession / Art, Memory / Shelter, Design / Analysis, Language / Action, Eclecticism / Classicism —Tamburelli suggests that there are no rules in architecture anymore, only policies and options.

4. On history

The artist Philip Guston once commented that when you begin working on a painting, there are a lot of people in the studio with you—your teachers, friends, family, painters from history, critics—but one by one they leave and, eventually, if you're lucky, you leave too.

I can imagine the creative process in Tamburelli's *Grundkurs* being not unlike the one described by Guston. When you begin you can feel the presence of the history of architecture in the studio, you can tell that Bramante was there, Claude Perrault was there, Schinkel was there, Fischer von Erlach was there, Hilberseimer was there, Hannes Meyer was there, Carl Andre was there, Aldo Rossi was there. But one by one, they will leave the studio, and all that will be left, hopefully, is the work that speaks of this historical lineage while remaining of its own; an independence evolved through erudition.

What Tamburelli has compiled from history is a curated image bank—a visual savings account that funds the design work. This is particularly poignant at a time when many architects remain reluctant to consider what they do as being part of a general cultural production, part of history, still insisting that their work is unprecedented and unrelated to past architectures. Aldo van Eyck summed up this attitude succinctly when he observed, "I have heard it said that an architect cannot be a prisoner of tradition in a time of change." For Van Eyck, the human condition—and with it, the essential task of architecture—was unchanging. He added, "It seems to me that [the architect] cannot be a prisoner of any kind. And at no time can he be a prisoner of change."

5. On process

Immersed in the Tudor revival of the late nineteenth century, Edwin Lutyens, at the age of thirty-five, began to indulge in neoclassicism. Pondering on the classical discipline, he wrote "That time-worn Doric Order—a lovely thing—I have the cheek to adopt. You can't copy it. To be right you have to take it and design it. . . . You cannot copy: you find if you do you are caught, a mess remains. It means hard labour, hard thinking, over every line in all three dimensions and in every joint; and no stone can be allowed to slide. If you tackle it in this way, the Order belongs to you, and every stroke, being mentally handled, must become endowed with such poetry and artistry as God has given you. You alter one feature (which you have to, always), then every other feature has to sympathise and undergo some care and invention. Therefore it is no mean [game], nor is it a game you can play lightheartedly."

The design process is a long journey, and often a struggle. While the destination might be already known from the start, the "hard labor" required to reach it changes the very nature and understanding of that destination, just as Lutyens learned from the Doric column.

Tamburelli's *Grundkurs* could be understood as a roadmap for such a journey, where the end is less critical than the process by which you get there.

As Lutyens's contemporary T. S. Eliot wrote, "We shall never cease from exploration and the end of all our exploring will be to arrive where we started and know the place for the first time."

6. On language

Adolf Loos gave a lot thought to the language of architecture. Within the context of the Vienna Secession and Wiener Werkstätte, he argued for a radical form of deradicalization—for normal to be the new avant-garde. Favoring evolution over revolution, iteration over innovation, he did not rethink every detail from scratch, a belief echoed many decades later by Charles Eames, who said "Innovate as a last resort. More horrors are done in the name of innovation than any other." Against the modernist ethos, Loos believed in an architectural language that did not speculate on how form and culture should appear in the future. By striving to be spectacularly unspectacular, Loos deployed a basic and comprehensible alphabet of architecture, a common grammar at a time when there was a Babel of creativity everywhere.

Tamburelli's *Grundkurs* shares Loos's disposition of a measured positivism. The images adopt a common alphabet for a visual language that is both erudite and accessible, while the text tends to be concise and aphoristic, understanding that the strength of the normal image and normal statement is a conduit for something innovative, something spectacular, and even something new, to emerge.

Loos embraced progress as long as it was situated within a larger cultural tradition, a position perhaps best articulated by Hermann Czech when he stated that "In order to communicate new ideas, one cannot use a new language at the same time." In the same vein, Tamburelli's *Grundkurs* projects an optimism for the future veiled behind a facade of the quotidian.

7. On pace

Scandinavia's embrace of Nordic classicism in the early twentieth century delayed the arrival of modernism, but when it did arrive, it was all the more refined and mature. At a time when the world moves at breakneck speed, being slow has its advantages.

While an academic or professional career can be forged at an accelerated pace, a more common phenomenon nowadays, when there is a disconnect between age and professional success, is to establish a deliberately slow pace, allowing time to absorb and digest before regurgitating. These slow-burn architects tend to be very good, very serious, while pursuing their own architectural interests with tenacity, quirkiness, and confidence. Free of the need to keep up with the latest microtrends, their work is quietly subversive.

Culture is fast, and getting faster and faster. Architecture is intrinsically slow, held back by all the capital, resources, and bureaucracy necessary for its realization. Rather than attempting to accelerate architecture to catch up with the pace of culture, Tamburelli's *Grundkurs* instills a counter position of slow deliberation to take advantage of the inevitable pace of architecture.

Even Tamburelli's act of drawing over images found on the internet signifies the act of making room for contemplation that this deliberate slowness brings to the design process. As John Hejduk wrote: "There is a short-distance runner architect and there is a long-distance runner architect . . . The short-distance runner is just that, a short-distance runner. His trail is straight, flat, and the end can be seen. He is a crowd pleaser. He runs fast and is soon out of breath. The long-distance runner's scope is simply vaster. He traverses a more complex landscape. He gets better with age, his distance is extended; his architecture at once becomes sparser and richer."

8. On positions

Oscar Wilde wrote that there are two kinds of artists: one of them supplies answers, the other asks questions. He stressed the necessity of knowing which category you belong to; for the one who asks questions is never the one who answers them.

Does the *Grundkurs* attempt to ask questions or give answers? Is it closer to the genre of investigative journalism or the genre of the manifesto? Tamburelli's seeming reluctance to enter into any kind of debate about what the lessons mean, claiming they are nothing more than an open-ended and deliberately non-exhaustive introduction to the discipline, betrays a conceptual stance that is much more rigorous than it may at first seem. Here, the combination of an elusive theoretical foundation and an insistence on structure and format means that each reciprocally debases and redeems the other. The deflection from definition—from providing a direct answer to the question "What is Architecture about?"—allows the *Grundkurs* to pose questions while at the same time insinuating answers.

This non-commitment to an overriding concept allows others to project their own meaning onto the *Grundkurs*, skillfully getting around the pitfall described by Borges: "God must not engage in theology. The writer must not destroy by human reasonings the faith that art requires of us."

Norman Foster,
Stansted Airport, 1991

Giovan Battista Piranesi, Ruins
of the Forum of Augustus,
Vedute di Roma, 1755

Antonio Averlino or
Filarete, Adam, ca. 1465

Hans Weiditz, Romulus
and Remus, ca. 1530

Edgard Degas, The Star, or
Dancer on stage, 1878

Andrea di Bonaiuto, Way of
Salvation, Spanish Chapel,
Santa Maria Novella, Florence,
ca. 1365–67

Ferdinand Dutert, Galerie des
Machines, Paris, 1889

Giovan Battista Piranesi,
Foundations of the Theatre
of Marcellus, Antichità
Romane, 1756

Centre George Pompidou under
construction, Paris, ca. 1975

Statue of Ramses, Abu Simbel,
Reconstruction, 1964–68

Gordon Matta Clark, Conical
Intersect, Paris, 1975

Renzo Piano, Richard Rogers,
Centre George Pompidou,
Paris, 1977

Temple of Hera II, Paestum,
5th century BC

Akira Kurosawa, Ran, 1985

National Gallery under
construction, Berlin, ca. 1965

Lilly Reich and Ludwig Mies
van der Rohe, Café Samt &
Seide, Berlin, 1927

Ludwig Mies van der Rohe,
National Gallery, Berlin, 1968

Roman Theatre, Orange,
1st century AD

Renzo Piano, De Menil
Foundation, Houston, 1986

Luis Barragán, Cuadra
San Cristobal, Atizapán
de Zaragoza, 1968

Claude Perrault, Ordonnance for
the Five Kinds of Columns, 1683

Adolf Loos, proposal for
the Chicago Tribune
Headquarters, 1922

William Chambers,
Rustic Building of conical
and Cubical Form, 1757

Donato Bramante,
Rustic Column, Canonica
di Sant'Ambrogio,
Milan, ca. 1492

Andrea Mantegna,
St. Sebastian, ca. 1480

Domenico Ghirlandaio, Visitation,
Tornabuoni Chapel, Santa Maria
Novella, Florence, ca. 1490

Antonello da Messina,
St. Sebastian, ca. 1478

Berlin Wall, ca. 1965

Wedding at Berlin Wall, ca. 1970

Archizoom, No-Stop City, 1969

Superstudio, Monumento
Continuo, 1969

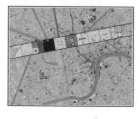

Office for Metropolitan
Architecture, Exodus, 1972

Ivan Leonidov, project for
the Lenin Institute, 1927

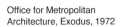

Office for Metropolitan
Architecture, Exodus, 1972

Ivan Leonidov, project for
the Lenin Institute, 1927

Rem Koolhaas, Laurinda Spear,
Villa in Miami, 1975

Le Corbusier, Beistegui attic,
Paris, 1932

Francesco di Giorgio, Terrace,
Palazzo Ducale, Urbino, ca. 1475

Luciano Laurana, Francesco di
Giorgio, Palazzo Ducale, Urbino,
ca. 1465–80

Giorgio Grassi, Restoration of
the Roman theatre, rear facade,
Sagunto, 1990

Giorgio Grassi, Restoration of the
Roman theatre, Sagunto, 1990

Ludwig Mies van der Rohe,
project for Resor house,
Jackson Hole, Wyoming, 1939

Giotto, Annunciation to
St. Anne, Scrovegni chapel,
Padua, 1303–05

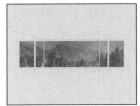

Ludwig Mies van der Rohe,
project for Resor house,
Jackson Hole, Wyoming, 1939

Kazuo Shinohara, Tanikawa
house, Nagano, 1972

Thomas Struth, photograph
of the Cathedral, Milan, 1998

Ludwig Mies van der Rohe,
National Gallery, Berlin, 1968

Thomas Struth, photograph of
Miletus Market Gate, Pergamon
Museum, Berlin, 1998

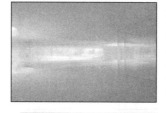

SAANA, Museum of Glass,
Toledo, Ohio, 2006

Gottfried Semper, Karl von
Hasenauer, Kunsthistorisches
Museum Vienna, 1891

Le Corbusier, Villa Stein,
Garches, 1927

Adolf Loos, Haus am
Michaelerplatz, 1912

Le Corbusier, kitchen, Villa
Savoy, Poissy, 1931

Adolf Loos, Lina Loos
Bedroom, Vienna, 1903

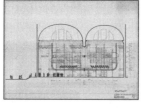

Renzo Piano, Section of
Prometeo Musical Space at
San Lorenzo, Venice, 1984

Donato Bramante, Project
for St. Peter's, 1506

Renzo Piano, Prometeo
Musical Space at San
Lorenzo, Venice, 1984

Alvaro Siza, Swimming Pool
at Leça da Palmeira, 1966

Domenico Fontana, Della
Trasportazione dell'Obelisco
Vaticano, 1590

Office for Metropolitan
Architecture, Project
of Convention Centre,
Agadir, 1990

Archigram, Walking Cities, 1964

Giovambattista Nolli,
Map of Rome, 1748

Geological Section

Map of Manhattan, 1807

Acropolis, Athens

Deir el-Bahari, Funerary Temple
of Queen Hatshepsut

Sancturary of Delphi,
plan, 5th century BC

Luxor Temple, plan,
16th century BC

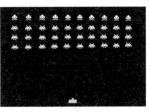

Tomohiro Nishikado,
Space Invaders, 1978

Pong, Superelectron TV
Challenger Series, Atari, 1977

Description de l'Égypte,
Karnak, 1809–29

Description de l'Égypte,
Karnak, 1809–29

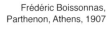

Frédéric Boissonnas,
Parthenon, Athens, 1907

Description de l'Égypte,
Abydos, 1809–29

Pheidias, Horse Head,
Parthenon, Eastern
Pediment, 438–432 BC

Hieroglyphs

Acropolis, Athens

Sanctuary of Fortune
at Palestrina

Parthenon, plan with
superimposed plans of
older and later temple

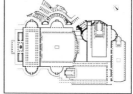

Imperial Fora, Rome

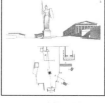

Auguste Choisy, Diagram of
the Acropolis of Athens, 1899

Raphael, School of Athens,
ca. 1509–11

Bas Princen, photograph
of Bramante's Santa Maria
delle Grazie, 2014

Temple of Heracles, Agrigento,
6th century BC

Adolf Loos, Proposal for the
Ringstrasse in Vienna, 1912

Renzo Piano, De Menil
Foundation, Houston, 1986

Giovan Battista Piranesi,
View of the Masso dei Metelli,
Le Antichità Romane, 1756–57

Citadel, Aleppo

Pier Paolo Pasolini, Medea, 1969

Charles Eisen for Marc-Antoine
Laugier, Frontispiece of the
Essai sur l'Architecture, 1755

Bent Pyramid, Dahshur,
27th century BC

Le Corbusier, Villa
Stein, Garches, 1927

Le Corbusier, Assembly
Building, Chandigarh, 1966

Antonio Averlino or
Filarete, Adam, ca. 1465

Plan of Msumba, Lunda empire

Steven Spielberg, Close
Encounters of the Third
Kind, 1977

Space suit, ca. 1970

Steven Spielberg, Close
Encounters of the Third
Kind, 1977

Steven Spielberg, Close
Encounters of the Third
Kind, 1977

Experimental room for space
travel training, ca. 1970

Gerhard Richter,
Niagara Falls, 1965

Experimental room for space
travel training, ca. 1960

Johann Bernhard Fischer
von Erlach, Nile Waterfalls,
Entwurff einer historischen
Architektur, 1721

Experimental installation for
space travel training, ca. 1960

Hagia Sophia, Istanbul

Kurt Schwitters, Merzbau,1923

Adolf Loos, proposal
for the Chicago Tribune
Headquarters, 1922

Aldo Rossi, Monument to
Resistance, Segrate, 1965

Raul Carapinha, Estufa
Fria, Lisbon, 1933

Ludwig Mies van der Rohe,
National Gallery, Berlin, 1968

Archigram, Instant
City, 1968–70

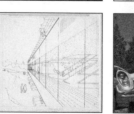

Mount Rushmore, 1927

Cedric Price, Project for
the Potteries Thinkbelt,
Staffordshire, 1964–66

Alfred Hitchcock, North
by Northwest, 1959

Grimshaw Architects,
Eden Project, the Biomes,
Cornwall, 1996–2000

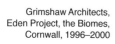

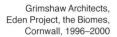

Grimshaw Architects,
Eden Project, the Biomes,
Cornwall, 1996–2000

Cedric Price, Aviary,
London Zoo, 1961–65

Berthold Lubetkin, Penguin
Pool, London Zoo, 1934

Akira Kurosawa, Ran, 1985

Temple of Hera II, Paestum,
5th century BC

Oktoberfest, Munich, ca. 2000

Description de l'Égypte,
Abydos, 1809–29

Derek Jarman, Prospect
Cottage, Dungeness, 1987

Deir el-Bahari, Funerary Temple
of Queen Hatshepsut

Derek Jarman, Prospect
Cottage, Dungeness, 1987

Deir el-Bahari, Funerary Temple
of Queen Hatshepsut

Deir el-Bahari, Funerary Temple
of Queen Hatshepsut

Deir el-Bahari, Funerary Temple
of Queen Hatshepsut

Ancient Egyptian Tombs
seen from the Nile

Ancient Egyptian Tombs
looking at the Nile

Andreas Gursky, photograph of
Theben West (Deir el-Bahari),
1993

Description de l'Égypte,
Pyramids at Giza, 1809–29

Bas Princen, photograph
of Sanctuary of Fortune at
Palestrina, 2014

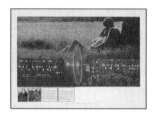

Superstudio, Fundamental
Acts: Love, 1971–75

Sanctuary of Fortune at
Palestrina, reconstruction
model according to Fasolo
and Gullini, 1953

Sanctuary of Fortune at
Palestrina, axonometry
according to Kähler, 1958

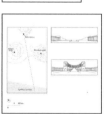

Sanctuary of Fortune at
Palestrina, relations to territory
after Fasolo Gullini, 1953

Archizoom, Dressing Design,
Nearest Habitat System, 1971

Pullarius (Roman Chicken Priest)

Roman ritual calendar
from Sabbatucci, 1988

Valie Export, Aktionshose:
Genitalpanik, 1969

Suovetaurilia, basrelief,
1st century AD

Kisho Kurokawa, capsule

Templum in terra

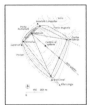

Kisho Kurokawa, Nagakin
Capsule Tower, 1970–72

Templum in aere superimposed
on Palatine Hill

Rome, seven hills

Italo Gismondi, Model
of Rome at the age of
Constantine, 1935–71

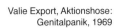

Walter Pichler, Inflatable
structure, 1966–69

Giovan Battista Piranesi, Circus
Maximus, Della Magnificenza e
Architettura dei Romani, 1761

Walter Pichler, Kleiner
Raum, Prototyp, 1966–69

Giovanna Silva, Photograph
of Circus Maximus, 2007

Anhangabaú Valley, São Paulo

View of viaduct over Anhangabaú,
São Paulo, 1878

View of Anhangabaú Valley,
São Paulo, 1927

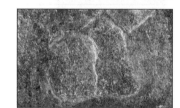

Vehicle Assembly Building,
Cape Canaveral

Black Stone

Pantheon, Rome

Kaaba without Kiswah (black
cloth), Masjid Al Haram, Mecca

Kaaba, Masjid Al Haram, Mecca

Le Corbusier, Vers une
Architecture, 1923

Giorgio Grassi, Antonio
Monestiroli, Student Housing
in Chieti, 1979

Fischli and Weiss, Popular
Opposites: Theory and Praxis,
1981–2012

Le Corbusier, Vers une
Architecture, 1923

Le Corbusier, Vers une
Architecture, 1923

Le Corbusier, Vers une
Architecture, 1923

Charles Eisen for Marc-Antoine
Laugier, Frontispiece of the
Essai sur l'Architecture, 1755

Philippe Starck, Asahi
Beer Hall, Tokyo, 1989

Office for Metroopolitan
Architecture, Proposal for
Zeebrugge Sea Terminal, 1988

Kaspar Friedrich Schinkel,
Gothic Cathedral
by a River, 1813

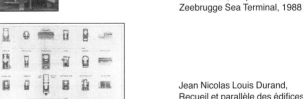

Jean Nicolas Louis Durand,
Recueil et parallèle des édifices
de tout genre anciens et
modernes, 1801

Friedrich Weinbrenner, Lange
Strasse, Karlsruhe, 1808

Giorgio Grassi, Antonio
Monestiroli, Student Housing
in Chieti, 1979

Heinrich Tessenow, Regional
School, Klotzsche, 1925

Giorgio Grassi, Antonio
Monestiroli, Student
Housing in Chieti, 1979

Kraftwerk, The Model, 1978

Big Black, Songs
About Fucking, 1987

Karl Friedrich Schinkel,
Proposal for the Mausoleum
of Queen Luise, 1810

Cesare Cesariano, Section
of Milan Cathedral, 1521

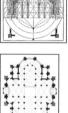

Plan of Milan Cathedral

Sanctuary of Fortune
at Palestrina

Sanctuary of Fortune at
Palestrina, axonometry
according to Kähler, 1958

Belvedere as analyzed
in Codex Coner

Paul Letarouilly, Plan and
Elevations of Bramante's
Belvedere

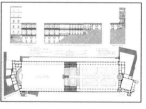

Pantheon and Basilica
of Maxentius

Sebastiano Serlio, Elevation
and Section of Bramante's
project for the Dome of
St. Peter's, 1544

Cake for 500th Anniversary
of Bramante's Death (baked
by San Rocco)

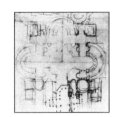

Donato Bramante, Project
for St. Peter's, 1506

Baldassarre Peruzzi,
Axonometry of St. Peter's
as of ca. 1514

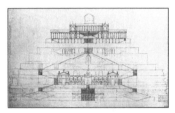

Andrea Palladio,
Redentore, 1592

Andrea Palladio, Reconstruction
of Sanctuary of Fortuna at
Palestrina, ca. 1560

Andrea Palladio, Reconstruction
of Sanctuary of Fortuna at
Palestrina, ca. 1560

Pietro da Cortona,
Reconstruction of Sanctuary
of Fortuna at Palestrina,
ca. 1636

Pietro da Cortona, Santi
Martina e Luca, 1650

Pietro da Cortona,
Reconstruction of Sanctuary
of Fortuna at Palestrina,
ca. 1636

Jacopo Barozzi da
Vignola, Palazzo Farnese,
Caprarola, 1599

Jacques Lemercier,
Drawing of Palazzo Farnese,
Caprarola, 1608

Jacopo Barozzi da
Vignola, Palazzo Farnese,
Caprarola, 1599

Le Corbusier, Cité de
Refuge, Paris, 1933

Le Corbusier, Studies for
Palace of Soviets, 1928–31

Le Corbusier, Cité de
Refuge, Paris, 1933

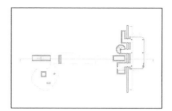

John Hejduk, Wall House, 1973

James Stirling, Proposal
for Siemens Headquarters,
Munich, 1969

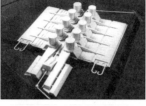

Stirling and Gowan, Faculty of
Engineering, Leicester, 1959

James Stirling, Staatsgalerie,
Stuttgart, 1984

James Stirling, axonometry of
central spaces of Staatsgalerie
Stuttgart, 1984

James Stirling, axonometry
of circulation of Staatsgalerie
Stuttgart, 1984

Bas Princen, photograph of
James Stirling's Olivetti Training
School, Haselmere, 1972

Bas Princen, photograph
of James Stirling's Florey
Building, Oxford, 1971

Bas Princen, photograph of
James Stirling's Faculty of
History, Cambridge, 1968

Bas Princen, photograph of
Stirling and Gowan's, Faculty of
Engineering, Leicester, 1959

James Stirling, Roma
Interrotta, 1978

Office for Metropolitan
Architecture, Exodus, 1972

Wedding at Berlin Wall, ca. 1970

Office for Metropolitan
Architecture, Parc de
la Villette, 1982

Section of Downtown
Athletic Club

Denise Scott Brown, Robert
Venturi, poster for Learning
from Las Vegas, 1972

Denise Scott Brown
in Las Vegas, 1966

Robert Venturi in Las Vegas, 1966

Las Vegas, ca. 1960

Venturi Rauch & Scott
Brown, Basco Supermarket,
Philadelphia, 1976

Big Donut Drive-in, Los
Angeles, 1970

Venturi Rauch & Scott
Brown, Basco Supermarket,
Philadelphia, 1976

Adalberto Libera (and Curzio
Malaparte), Malaparte
house, Capri, 1937

Curzio Malaparte in Lipari, 1933

Jean-Luc Godard,
Le Mépris, 1963

Aldo Rossi, School in
Fagnano Olona, 1976

Luigi Ghirri, Gate in
Formigine, 1988

Aldo Rossi, Proposal for San
Nazaro dei Burgundi, 1967

Luigi Ghirri, Cittanova, 1980

Le Corbusier, La Tourette
Monastery, 1960

Le Corbusier, Vers une
Architecture, 1923

Le Corbusier, Note, 1963

Long Island Duck, 1964

Giotto, The Expulsion of
Joachim from the temple,
Scrovegni Chapel, Padua,
1303–05

Venturi and Scott Brown,
National Collegiate Football Hall
of Fame, New Brunswick, 1967

Venturi and Scott Brown,
National Collegiate Football Hall
of Fame, New Brunswick, 1967

Giotto, The Institution of the
Crib, Upper Basilica, Assisi,
ca. 1292–96

Enzo Mari, Hammer
and Sickle, 1973

Enzo Mari, Fourty-four
Evaluations, 1977

Enzo Mari, The Portrait
of God, 2001

Enzo Mari, The Portrait
of God, 2001

Enzo Mari, The Portrait
of God, 2001

Aldo Rossi, School, Broni, 1971

Aldo Rossi, Idea for a School,
Fagnano Olona, 1972

Aldo Rossi, School,
Fagnano Olona, 1972

Aldo Rossi, Idea for a
School, Broni, 1982

Aldo Rossi, Hotel, Fukuoka 1994

Giotto, The Expulsion of
Joachim from the Temple,
Scrovegni Chapel, Padua,
1303–05

Giotto, The Presentation of the
Virgin in the Temple, Scrovegni
Chapel, Padua, 1303–05

Taddeo Gaddi, The
Presentation of the Virgin
in the Temple, Scrovegni
Chapel, Padua, 1330

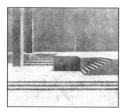

Charles Jencks, The
Language of Post-Modern
Architecture, 1977

Adolphe Appia, Tristan
and Isolde, 1923

Robert Bresson,
Pickpocket, 1959

Robert Bresson, Lancelot
du Lac, 1974

John Baldessari, Throwing
Three Balls in the Air to Get
a Straight Line, 1973

Roy Lichtenstein, Why Brad Darling, this Painting is a Masterpiece, 1962

John Baldessari, Four Portraits of Swords Aligned, 1976

George Baird, Charles Jencks, Meaning in Architecture, 1969

Giulio Paolini, Diaframma, 1965

Giulio Paolini, Diaframma, 1965

Cornelius Gysbrechts, The Reverse of a Framed Painting, 1670

Giulio Paolini, Diaframma, 1965

Giulio Minoletti, Eugenio Gentili Tedeschi, Proposal for Central Station, Milan, 1952

Giulio Minoletti, Eugenio Gentili Tedeschi, Proposal for Central Station, Milan, 1952

Giulio Minoletti, Eugenio Gentili Tedeschi, Proposal for Central Station, Milan, 1952

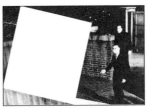

Giulio Minoletti, Eugenio Gentili Tedeschi, Proposal for Central Station, Milan, 1952

Ludovico Quaroni, Mario Ridolfi, Proposal for Termini Railway Station, Rome, 1947

Eugenio Montuori, Termini Railway Station, Rome, 1947–50

Ludovico Quaroni, Mario Ridolfi, Proposal for Termini Railway Station, Rome, 1947

Eugenio Montuori, Model of Termini Railway Station, Rome, 1947

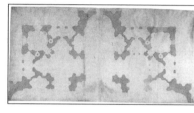

Adolf Loos, Proposal for the Chicago Tribune Headquarters, 1922

João Batista Vilanova Artigas, FAU-USP, São Paulo, 1969

Fra Giovanni Giocondo, Project for St. Peter's, 1506

Donato Bramante, Project for St. Peter's, 1506

Claude Nicolas Ledoux, Plan of Oikema, or House of Pleasure, 1780

Oswald Mathias Ungers, Plan of Regional Library, Karlsruhe, 1991

Oswald Mathias Ungers, Axonometry of Regional Library, Karlsruhe, 1991

Claude Nicolas Ledoux, View of Oikema, or House of Pleasure, 1780

Etienne Louis Boullée, View of Newton Cenotaph, 1764

Etienne Louis Boullée, Section of Newton Cenotaph, 1764

Etienne Louis Boullée, Proposal for National Library, 1785

Boris Iofan, Proposal for Palace of the Soviets, 1937

Raphael, School of Athens, ca. 1509–11

Hagia Sophia, Istanbul

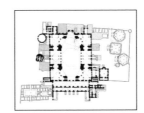

Plan of Hagia Sophia, Istanbul

Finding and Recognition of the
true Cross, San Francesco,
Arezzo, 1452–66

David Hockney, American
Collectors, 1968

Giotto, Resurrection of Drusiana,
Peruzzi Chapel, Santa Croce,
Florence, ca. 1320

Giotto, Resurrection of Drusiana,
Peruzzi Chapel, Santa Croce,
Florence, ca. 1320

Gunnar Erik Asplund, Public
Library, Stockholm, 1940

Sigurd Lewerentz, Resurrection
Chapel, Woodland Cemetery,
Stockholm, 1940

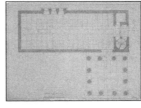

Alvaro Siza, Bonjour
Tristesse, Berlin, 1984

Sigurd Lewerentz, Plan of
Resurrection Chapel, Woodland
Cemetery, Stockholm, 1940

Sigurd Lewerentz, Situation
Plan of Resurrection Chapel,
Woodland Cemetery,
Stockholm, 1940

Johann Bernhard Fischer
von Erlach, City for Alexander
the Great on Mount Athos,
Entwurff einer historischen
Architektur, 1721

Olympia, View of Ruins

Map of Athens in
the Age of Pericles

Reconstruction of the Acropolis
of Athens in the age of Pericles

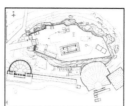

Plan of the Acropolis of Athens

View from Parthenon, Athens

View of Parthenon, Athens

View of Parthenon with
Tourists, Athens

Charles Eisen for Marc-Antoine Laugier, Frontispiece of the Essai sur l'Architecture, 1755

Giambattista Nolli, Map of Rome, 1748

Marc-Antoine Laugier, Essai sur l'Architecture, title page, 1755

Cesare Cesariano, Illustration for Vitruvius' De Architectura, Book II, XXXII, 1521

Daniel Defoe, The Life and Strange Surprising Adventures of Robinson Crusoe, of York, Mariner, title page, 1719

Marshall Sahlins, Stone Age Economics, book cover, 1974

Adam Smith, An Inquiry into the Nature and Causes of the Wealth of Nations, title page, 1776

Bronisław Malinowski, Argonauts of the Western Pacific, cover, 1922

Roland Fréart de Chambray, Kallimachos sketching a basket covering an acanthus plant (Origin of Corinthian Order), 1650

Ted Post, Beneath the Planet of the Apes, 1970

Franco Albini, Franca Helg, Bob Noorda, Massimo Vignelli, Metro Line 1, Milan, 1964

Aldo Rossi, L'architettura della Città, cover, 1966

Achille and Pier Giacomo Castiglioni, Montecatini pavilion National Exhibition of Agricultural Pesticides, 1955

Massimo Vignelli, Aldo Rossi staring at Josip Stalin's Portrait, Moscow, 1955

Portraits of Claude Levi Strauss and Adolf Loos

Luca Meda, Aldo Rossi, Bridge for XIII Triennale, Milan, 1964

Luca Meda, Aldo Rossi, Bridge for XIII Triennale, Milan, 1964

Mart Stam, Tubular Chair, 1927

Aldo Rossi, Monument to
Resistance, Segrate, 1965

Aldo Rossi, Proposal for San
Nazaro dei Burgundi, 1967

Cover of issue no.1 of ABC

Johann Bernhard Fischer
von Erlach, Entwurff einer
historischen Architektur,
title page, 1721

Hannes Meyer,
Co-op interior, 1926

Johann Bernhard Fischer von
Erlach, captions to Plate III,
Entwurff einer historischen
Architektur, 1721

Hannes Meyer, Co-op
construction, 1926

Felice Casorati, Eggs on
the Commode, 1920

Meyer Wittwer League Of
Nations Geneva Proposal

Della Francesca Pala
Di Brera Apsis

Christopher Alexander,
Notes on the Synthesis of
Form, book cover, 1964

Johann Bernhard Fischer
von Erlach, Hanging Gardens
of Babylon, Entwurff einer
historischen Architektur, 1721

Alain Resnais, Last Year
at Marienbad, 1961

Joseph Esherick, Lawrence
Halprin, Donlyn Lyndon,
Charles Moore, William
Turnbull, Richard Whitaker,
Sea Ranch, California, 1965

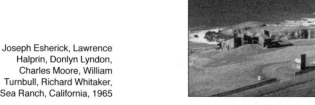

Anna Halprin, Dance Workshop
at Sea Ranch, ca. 1960

Robert Venturi, Complexity
and Contradiction in
Architecture, 1966

Robert Venturi, Complexity
and Contradiction in
Architecture, 1966

Canaletto, Rialto Bridge with
Palladian buildings, 1756–59

Robert Venturi, Complexity
and Contradiction in
Architecture, 1966

Johann Bernhard Fischer von
Erlach, Pyramids of Giza,
Entwurff einer historischen
Architektur, 1721

Gerhard Richter,
Pyramids of Giza, 1985

Cover of issue no. 3 of G, 1924

Johann Bernhard Fischer
von Erlach, Mausoleum at
Halicarnassus, Entwurff einer
historischen Architektur, 1721

Hans Kollhoff, Proposal for
Ethnographic Museum, 1982

Hans Kollhoff, Proposal for
Potsdamerplatz, 1993

Hans Kollhoff, Leibniz
Kolonnaden, Berlin, 2000

Johann Bernhard Fischer von Erlach, Colossus of Rhodes, Entwurff einer historischen Architektur, 1721

Johann Bernhard Fischer von Erlach, Nile Waterfalls, Entwurff einer historischen Architektur, 1721

Gerhard Richter, Niagara Falls, 1965

Inigo Jones, The Most Notable Antiquity of Great Britain, Vulgarly Called Stonehenge, title page, 1655

Johann Bernhard Fischer von Erlach, Stonehenge and Arch-shaped Rock near Salzburg, Entwurff einer historischen Architektur, 1721

Inigo Jones, The Most Notable Antiquity of Great Britain, Vulgarly Called Stonehenge, 1655

Madelon Vriesendorp, The Arrival of the Floating Pool, 1975

Johann Bernhard Fischer von Erlach, Isola Bella on Lake Maggiore, Entwurff einer historischen Architektur, 1721

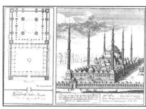

Johann Bernhard Fischer von Erlach, Sultan Ahmed Mosque, Entwurff einer historischen Architektur, 1721

Johann Bernhard Fischer von Erlach, Mosque in Mecca, Entwurff einer historischen Architektur, 1721

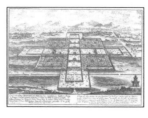

Johann Bernhard Fischer von Erlach, Forbidden City in Beijing, Entwurff einer historischen Architektur, 1721

Johann Bernhard Fischer von Erlach, Pagoda in Nanking, Entwurff einer historischen Architektur, 1721

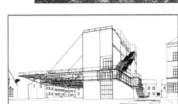

Ludwig Hilberseimer, Proposal of New Blocks for Friedrichstadt, Berlin, 1928

Italo Gismondi, Model of Rome at the age of Constantine, 1935–71

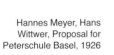

Hannes Meyer, Hans Wittwer, Proposal for Peterschule Basel, 1926

Ludwig Mies van der Rohe, Proposal for Reichsbank, rear facade, 1933

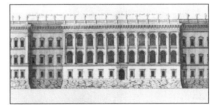

Hyacinthe Rigaud, Portrait of Louis XIV, 1701

Gian Lorenzo Bernini, Third Proposal for the Louvre, 1665

Philippe de Champaigne, Portrait of Jean-Baptiste Colbert, 1655

Giovanni Battista Gaulli, Portrait of Gian Lorenzo Bernini, 1665

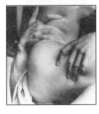

Gian Lorenzo Bernini, The Rape of Proserpina, 1621–22

Gian Lorenzo Bernini, Caricature of Innocent XI, 1676

Gian Lorenzo Bernini, Fountain of Four Rivers, Piazza Navona, Rome, 1651

Gian Lorenzo Bernini, St. Peter's Square, 1675

Gian Lorenzo Bernini, Portrait of Louis XIV, 1665

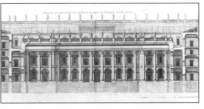

Gian Lorenzo Bernini, Third Proposal for the Louvre, Section, 1665

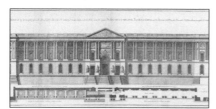

Claude Perrault, South-eastern
Facade of the Louvre
Palace, 1667

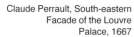

Gian Lorenzo Bernini, Third
Proposal for the Louvre,
South-western Facade
along the River, 1665

Charles Le Brun, Ordre
Francisas for the Galerie
des Glaces, 1681–84

Henry Latrobe,
American Order, 1809

Henry Latrobe,
American Order, 1809

Renzo Piano, Richard
Rogers, Centre George
Pompidou, Paris, 1977

Ieoh Ming Pei, Pyramid,
Louvre, 1989

Ezra Stoller, Interior of
Skidmore, Owings & Merrill's
Inland Steel Building,
Chicago, 1958

August Sander, Portrait
of Hans Poelzig, 1928

Portrait of Charles McKim,
William Mead and Stanford
White, ca. 1905

Portrait of Zaha Hadid, ca. 2010

Cecil B. De Mille, The Ten
Commandements, 1956

Workers at construction site
for World Cup Qatar 2022

IKEA logistic platform,
Piacenza, 2007

João Batista Vilanova Artigas,
FAU-USP, São Paulo, 1969

Klaus Kinsky as Aguirre
in Werner Herzog's Aguirre,
the Wrath of God, 1972

Donato Bramante, Project
for St. Peter's, 1506

Rex Harrison as Julius II
and Harry Andrews as
Bramante in Carol Reed's The
Agony and the Fury, 1965

Gary Cooper as Howard
Roark in King Vidor's The
Fountainhead, 1949

René Burri, Le Corbusier
discussing La Tourette
Monastery with Dominican
Fathers, 1959

Le Corbusier, Idea for
Addis Ababa, 1936

Gian Lorenzo Bernini, Francesco
Borromini, St. Peter's Baldachin,
1623–34

Gian Lorenzo Bernini, Francesco Borromini, St. Peter's Baldachin, 1623–34

Giovanni Giacomo De Rossi, Ceremony of Canonization of St. Francis de Sales in St. Peter's, 1665

Gian Lorenzo Bernini, Francesco Borromini, St. Peter's Baldachin, detail, 1623–34

Gian Lorenzo Bernini, Francesco Borromini, St. Peter's Baldachin, list and measurements of golden elements, 1623–34

Gian Lorenzo Bernini, Francesco Borromini, St. Peter's Baldachin, detail, 1623–34

Gian Lorenzo Bernini, Francesco Borromini, St. Peter's Baldachin, list and measurements of golden elements, 1623–34

Gian Lorenzo Bernini, Francesco Borromini, St. Peter's Baldachin, detail, 1623–34

Vincent De Rijk making model of OMA's Zeebrugge Terminal proposal, 1988

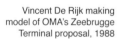

OMA, Model studies for Zeebrugge Terminal, 1988

Vincent De Rijk making model of OMA's Zeebrugge Terminal proposal, 1988

OMA, Model studies for Zeebrugge Terminal, 1988

Gian Lorenzo Bernini, Scala Regia, plan and section, 1663–66

Gian Lorenzo Bernini, Scala Regia, 1663–66

Giovan Battista Tiepolo, Portrait of Balthasar Neumann, detail of fresco above the main staircase of Würzburg Residenz, 1752–53

Portrait of Hannes Meyer, ca. 1920

Cover of issue no.1 of ABC

Hans Schmidt, Paul Artaria,
Huber house, Basel, 1929

Hans Schmidt, Paul Artaria,
Schaeffer house, Basel, 1929

Max Bill, Rote Strahlung, 1959

Hannes Meyer, Hans Wittwer,
Proposal for League of Nations
Headquaters, 1927

Hannes Meyer, Hans Wittwer,
Proposal for League of Nations
Headquaters, 1927

Le Corbusier, Proposal
for League of Nations
Headquaters, 1927

Le Corbusier, Proposal
for League of Nations
Headquaters, 1927

Hans Poelzig, Proposal
for League of Nations
Headquaters, 1927

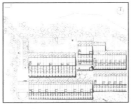

Atelier 5, Housing
Halen, Bern, 1961

Atelier 5, Plan of Housing
Halen, Bern, 1961

Atelier 5, Housing
Halen, Bern, 1961

Skidmore, Owings & Merrill,
Lever House, New York, 1952

Ludwig Mies van der
Rohe, Seagram Building,
New York, 1958

Group picture with all
architects involved in
Chicago World Fair, 1893

Portrait of Louis Sullivan,
ca. 1900

Portrait of Frank Lloyd
Wright, ca. 1950

McKim, Mead & White,
Pennsylvania Station, New
York, 1910 (demolished 1963)

Daniel Burnham, Flatiron,
New York, 1902

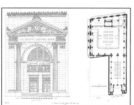

McKim, Mead & White,
Plan of Bovery Savings
Bank, New York, 1895

Norman Mailer as Stanford
White in Milos Forman's
Ragtime, 1981

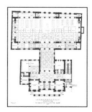

McKim, Mead & White, Plan
of Bank of Montreal, 1904

Robert Joy as Harry Kendall
Thaw in Milos Forman's
Ragtime, 1981

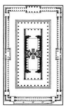

Ruins of temple of
Venus and Rome

Plan of Temple of Venus and
Rome, 2nd century AD

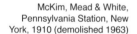

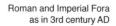

Roman and Imperial Fora
as in 3rd century AD

Luigi Canina, Reconstruction
of Temple of Venus and
Rome, 1841

Skidmore, Owings & Merrill (Gordon Bunshaft), Pepsi Cola Headquarters, New York, 1958

Robert Venturi, Plan of proposal for Transportation Square Office Building, Washington, 1968

Skidmore, Owings & Merrill (Gordon Bunshaft), Pepsi Cola Headquarters, New York, 1958

Robert Venturi, Model of Proposal for Transportation Square Office Building, Washington, 1968

Eero Saarinen, Kevin Roche, John Deere Headquarters, 1963

Cesar Pelli, Pacific Design Center, Los Angeles, 1975

Ed Ruscha, War Surplus, 1962

Cesar Pelli, Pacific Design Center, Los Angeles, 1975

Frank O. Gehry, Gehry House, Santa Monica, 1977

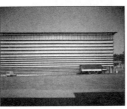

Herzog & de Meuron, Ricola Storage, Laufen, 1986

Herzog & de Meuron, Ricola Storage, Laufen, 1986

Martin Ries, Carl Andre installing work, 1964

Herzog & de Meuron, Ricola Storage, Laufen, 1986

Carl Andre at Whitechapel Gallery, London, 1978

Guerrilla Girls, What Do These Men Have in Common?, 1995

Herzog & de Meuron,
Apartment Building in
Hebelstrasse, Basel, 1988

Gerhard Richter,
Motorboat, 1965

Herzog & de Meuron,
Apartment Building in
Hebelstrasse, Basel, 1988

Herzog & de Meuron,
Apartment Building in
Hebelstrasse, Basel, 1988

Luisa Lambri, photograph of
Oscar Niemeyer's Canoas
House, 2003

Richard Meier, Douglas House,
Harbor Springs, 1973

Cordoba Mosque,
8th–10th century AD

Qasr Al-Mshatta, Detail of
facade, 8th century AD

Qasr Al-Mshatta, 8th century AD

Portrait of Keppel Archibald
Cameron Creswell

Mosaic, Sant'Apollinare
Nuovo, 561,

Mosaic, Great Mosque,
Damascus, 708–715 AD

Great Mosque of Damascus,
708–715 AD

Great Mosque of Damascus,
708–715 AD

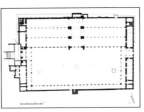

Great Mosque of Damascus,
708–715 AD

Great Mosque of Samarra,
848–851 AD

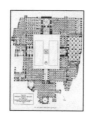

Jameh Mosque, Isfahan,
7th–15th century AD

Great Mosque, Kairouan,
7th–9th century AD

Jameh Mosque, Isfahan,
7th–15th century AD

Great Mosque, Medina,
from 7th century

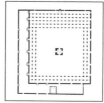

Mosque of Ibn Tulun,
Cairo, 876–879

Mosque of Ibn Tulun,
Cairo, 876–879

Mosque of Ibn Tulun,
Cairo, 876–879

Lewis Gilbert, The Spy
Who Loved Me, 1977

Lewis Gilbert, The Spy
Who Loved Me, 1977

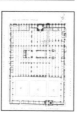

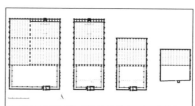

Cordoba Mosque, Plan

Diagram showing the evolution
of the Cordoba Mosque

Le Corbusier, Palace of
Assembly, Chandigarh, 1962

Le Corbusier, Palace of
Assembly, Chandigarh, 1962

OMA, Proposal for Convention
Centre, Agadir, 1990

Portrait of Ludwig Hilbersheimer

Ludwig Hilberseimer, Proposal for Chicago Tribune, 1922

Ludwig Hilberseimer, Alfred Caldwell, Studies for the Chicago Area, 1942

Irenio Diotallevi, Francesco Marescotti, Città orizzontale, Milan, 1940

Adalberto Libera, Unità di Abitazione Orizzontale, Rome, 1950–54

Adalberto Libera, Unità di Abitazione Orizzontale, Rome, 1950–54

Adalberto Libera, Unità di Abitazione Orizzontale, Rome, 1950–54

Jacobus Johannes Pieter Oud, De Kiefhoek, Rotterdam, 1930

Jacobus Johannes Pieter Oud, De Kiefhoek, Rotterdam, 1930

Ludwig Hilbersheimer, Highrise City, 1924

Ludwig Mies van der Rohe, Reichsbank, 1933

Claude Perrault, Louvre, Paris, 1667–74

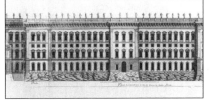

Gian Lorenzo Bernini, Project for the East Facade of the Louvre, Paris, 1665

Ludwig Mies van der Rohe,
Reichsbank, 1933

Ludwig Mies van der Rohe,
Proposal for a tower in
Friedrichstraße, 1921

Ludwig Mies van der Rohe,
Reichsbank, 1933

Ludwig Mies van der Rohe,
Proposal for a tower in
Friedrichstraße, 1921

Foster and Partners,
Willis Faber Dumas Building,
Ipswich, 1970–75

Foster and Partners,
Willis Faber Dumas Building,
Ipswich, 1970–75

Foster and Partners,
Willis Faber Dumas Building,
Ipswich, 1970–75

Foster and Partners,
Willis Faber Dumas Building,
Ipswich, 1970–75

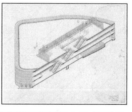

Foster and Partners,
Willis Faber Dumas Building,
Ipswich, 1970–75

Foster and Partners,
Willis Faber Dumas Building,
Ipswich, 1970–75

Raffaele Stern, Restoration
of Coliseum, Eastern
Buttress, 1806–07

Giuseppe Valadier, Restoration
of Coliseum, Western Buttress,
1823–26

Hans Döllgast, Restauration
of the Alte Pinakothek,
Munich, 1950

Giorgio Grassi, Library,
Groningen, 1990–92

Giorgio Grassi, Library,
Groningen, 1990–92

Giorgio Grassi,
Regional Administration
Building, Trieste, 1974

Giorgio Grassi, Library,
Groningen, 1990–92

Giorgio Grassi,
Regional Administration
Building, Trieste, 1974

Giorgio Grassi, Library,
Groningen, 1990–92

Giorgio Morandi, Still life, 1956

Frank Gehry, Indiana Avenue
Studios, Los Angeles, 1979–81

Giorgio Morandi, Still life, 1956

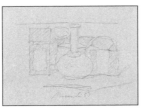

Frank Gehry, Indiana Avenue
Studios, Los Angeles, 1979–81

Philip Guston, Still life, 1970

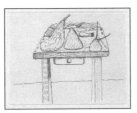

Philip Guston, Roma, 1971

Robert Venturi, North Penn
Visting Nurses' Association,
Amber, 1961

Philip Guston, Red Box, 1977

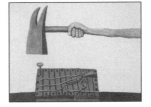

Alghiero Boetti, Map, 1978

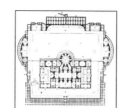

Caracalla Baths,
Rome, 2nd century AD

McKim, Mead & White,
Pennsylvania Station,
New York, 1902

McKim, Mead & White,
Pennsylvania Station,
New York, 1902

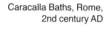

Caracalla Baths, Rome,
2nd century AD

McKim, Mead & White,
Pennsylvania Station,
New York, 1902

McKim, Mead & White,
Pennsylvania Station,
New York, 1902

Michele Sanmicheli, Palazzo
Grimani, Venice, 1556

McKim, Mead & White, Tiffany
Store Building, New York, 1906

Cass Gilbert, Woolworth Building, New York, 1913

Karl Friedrich Schinkel, Friedrichswerdersche Church, Berlin, 1824–31

Pablo Picasso, Two Women at a Bar, 1902

Gerhard Richter, Abstract Painting, 1999

Pablo Picasso, Boy Leading a Horse, 1906

Gerhard Richter, Motorboat, 1965

Andy Warhol, Oyster Stew, 1969

Sigmar Polke, Socks, 1963

Roy Lichtenstein, Whaam!, 1963

Gerhard Richter, Jet Fighter, 1963

Andrea Mantegna, The Triumph of Caesar, The Elephants, 1484–92

Raphael, The Fire at Borgo, Apostolic Palace, Vatican, 1514–17

Bill Parker standing in front of Dana Schutz's painting Open Casket at Whitney Biennial, 2017

Dana Schutz, Open Casket, 2016

Enzo Mari, Dialogue, 1986

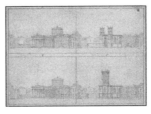

Karl Friedrich Schinkel, Four alternative projects for the Friedrichswerdersche Church, Berlin, 1824

Karl Friedrich Schinkel,
Friedrichswerdersche
Church, Berlin, 1824–31

Karl Friedrich Schinkel,
Friedrichswerdersche
Church, Berlin, 1824–31

Karl Friedrich Schinkel,
Friedrichswerdersche
Church, Berlin, 1824–31

Karl Friedrich Schinkel,
Friedrichswerdersche
Church, Berlin, 1824–31

Siegfried Giedion,
Fernand Léger, José
Lluís Sert, Nine Points on
Monumentality, 1943–58

Adolf Loos, Proposal for the
Chicago Tribune, 1922

Fernand Léger, Divers,
Mural, New York, 1942

Ludwig Mies van der Rohe,
Dominion Center, Toronto, 1967

Fernand Léger, Divers
at House W. K. Harrison,
New York City, 1942

Diego Rivera, Man at
the Crossroads, 1934

Ludwig Mies van der Rohe,
Dominion Center, Toronto, 1967

Stanley Tigerman, Black
Barn, Frog Hollow, 1973–74

James Stirling, Faculty of
History, Cambridge, 1968

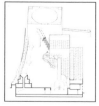

Stanley Tigerman, The
Titanic, Collage, 1978

James Stirling, Michael Wilford,
Wallraf Richartz Museum,
Cologne, Germany, 1975

Stanley Tigerman, Hotdog
House, Harvard, 1972–74

Stanley Tigerman, Hotdog
House, Harvard, 1972–74

James Stirling, Bookshop,
Venice, 1991

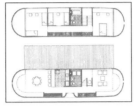

Stanley Tigerman, Hotdog
House, Harvard, 1972–74

James Stirling, Bookshop,
Venice, 1991

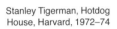

Andrea Palladio, Villa
Serego, Verona, 1560–70

Andrea Palladio, Villa
Serego, Verona, 1560–70

Jacopo Sansovino, Villa Garzoni,
Pontecasale, ca. 1540

Federico Zuccari, Palazzo
Zuccari, Rome, 1590–1610

Cesare Cesariano, Section
of Milan Cathedral, 1521

Pantheon and Basilica
of Maxentius

Antonio San Gallo the Younger
for Bramante, Corinthian Capital
for St. Peter's, ca. 1507

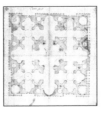

Giuliano da Sangallo, Project
for St. Peter's, ca. 1506

Donato Bramante, Corrections
to Giuliano da Sangallo's
Proposal for St. Peter's, ca. 1506

Jacopo Barozzi da Vignola,
Palazzo dei Banchi,
Bologna, 1565–68

Jacopo Barozzi da Vignola,
Sant'Andrea alla via Flaminia,
Rome, 1550

Villa Adriana, Tivoli,
ca. 118–134 AD

Villa Adriana, Tivoli,
ca. 118–134 AD

Ludwig Mies van der Rohe,
Villa Tugendhat, Brno, 1930

Salvador Dalí's House,
Portlligat, Spain, 1930

Hans Hollein, Travel Agency,
Vienna, 1976–78

Christian Jank, Eduard
Riedel, Georg von Dollmann,
Neuschwanstein Castle,
Bavaria, 1869

Castel del Monte, ca.1240

Carlo Mollino, Teatro
Regio, Turin, 1973

Castel del Monte, ca.1240

Leon Krier, Atlantis, 1986

John Nash, Royal Pavilion,
Brighton, 1827

Leon Krier, Atlantis, 1986

Karl Friedrich Schinkel, Zeltzimmer, Charlottenhof, Potsdam, ca. 1826

Boris Iofan, Moscow State University, Main Building, 1947

Giorgio Grassi, Biblioteca Comunale, Milan, 1990

Carlo Mollino, Teatro Regio, Turin, 1973

Anthony Mann, The Fall of the Roman Empire, 1964

Paul Klee, Main roads and side roads, 1929

Ilya Repin, Reply of the Zaporozhian Cossacks, 1880–91

Cartoon of Bolshevik leaders writing a letter to Lord Curzon, 1923

Vladimir Tatlin, Monument to the Third International, 1919–20

Werner Tübke, Early Bourgeois Revolution in Germany, Cyclorama, Bad Frankenhausen, 1976–87

Werner Tübke, Early Bourgeois Revolution in Germany, Cyclorama, Bad Frankenhausen, 1976–87

Gerhard Richter, Cow, 1964

Salvador Dalí, The Colossus of Rhodes, 1954

Werner Tübke presenting a 1:10 version of his painting to Erich Honecker

OMA, Proposal for Zeebrugge
Sea Terminal, 1988

OMA, Proposal for Zeebrugge
Sea Terminal, 1988

Donato Bramante, Santa
Maria presso San Satiro,
Milan, ca. 1480

Stanley Tigerman,
Illinois Regional Library for
the Blind and Physically
Handicapped, Chicago, 1978

James Stirling, Staatsgalerie
Stuttgart, Germany, 1977–84

Stanley Tigerman,
Illinois Regional Library for
the Blind and Physically
Handicapped, Chicago, 1978

Gunnar Birkerts, Public
Library, Duluth, USA, 1980

Acknowledgements

These lessons were held at TU Wien as part of the "Grundlagen des Entwerfens" course from September 2021 to January 2022. Ursula Aichner, Falck Joseph Oswald, Nadja Muck, and Thomas Sieberer helped me organize the lessons.

This version of the *Grundkurs* emerged in conversations with Inge Andritz, Anna Livia Friel, Ernst Pfaffeneder, Patrick Pregesbauer, Gerhard Schnabl, Adam Sherman, Manfred Walzer, and Klaus Zwerger, who work (or have worked) with me as the chair of "Gestaltungslehre and Design."

The images for the book have been collected and classified by Patrick Pregesbauer.

I would like to thank Pamela Johnston for supporting the idea of this book from the beginning, Mark Lee for his intriguing and erudite notes, Louis Rogers for his precious editorial suggestions, and Morgan Crowcroft-Brown for her elegant graphic design. This book would not have been possible without the enthusiasm of Michael Mack.

Finally, I would like to thank my daughter Delfina, who was often drawing next to me while I was preparing these lessons, and was never tempted to overwrite, erase, wet, eat, or burn any of my doodles.

Grundkurs: What is Architecture About?
Pier Paolo Tamburelli

First edition published by MACK
© 2023 MACK for this edition
© 2023 Pier Paolo Tamburelli for his sketches and text
© 2023 Mark Lee for his text

Text editor: Pamela Johnston
Project editor: Louis Rogers
Design: Morgan Crowcroft-Brown & Pier Paolo Tamburelli
Printed by KOPA, Lithuania

ISBN 978-1-913620-95-0
mackbooks.co.uk